Low-Cholesterol Diet Cookbook for Beginners

2000 Days of Heart-Healthy Habits and Easy, Quick Recipes with Simple Ingredients

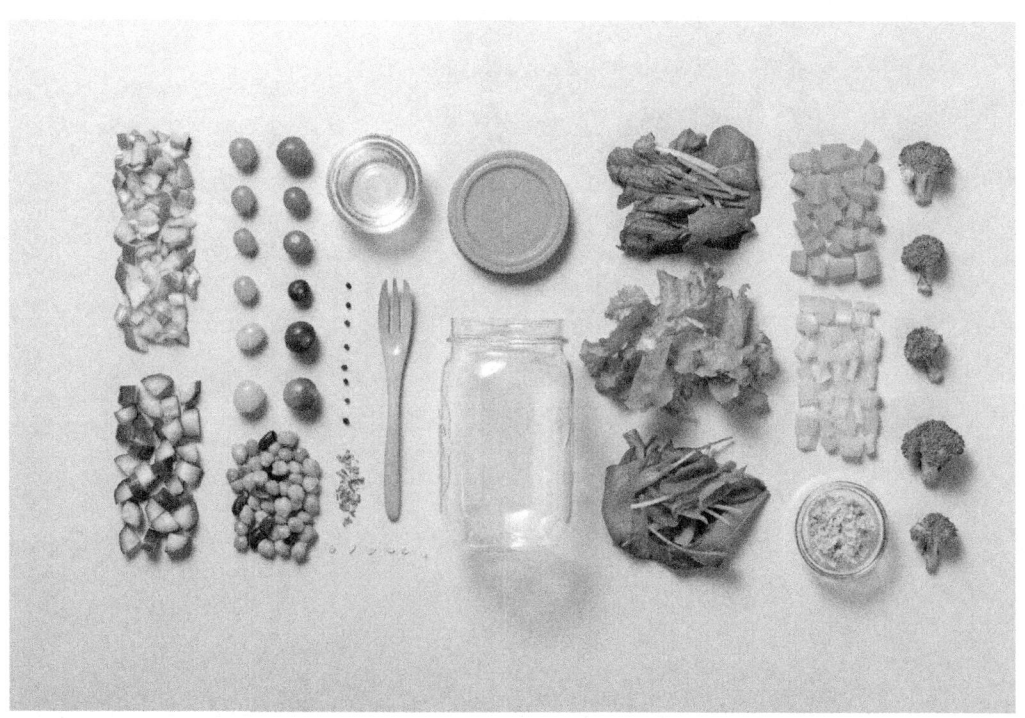

© 2024 by Ariana Elizabeth Montgomery. All rights reserved. No part of this publication may be reproduced, distributed, or transmitted in any form or by any means, including photocopying, recording, or other electronic or mechanical methods, without the prior written permission of the publisher, except in the case of brief quotations embodied in critical reviews and certain other noncommercial uses permitted by copyright law.

The material in this book is provided for educational and informational purposes only and is not intended as medical advice. The information contained in this book should not be used to diagnose or treat any illness, metabolic disorder, disease, or health problem. Always consult your physician or health care provider before beginning any nutrition or exercise program. The use of the advice in this book is at your own risk. The author and publisher of this book disclaim any liabilities or loss in connection with the exercises and advice herein.

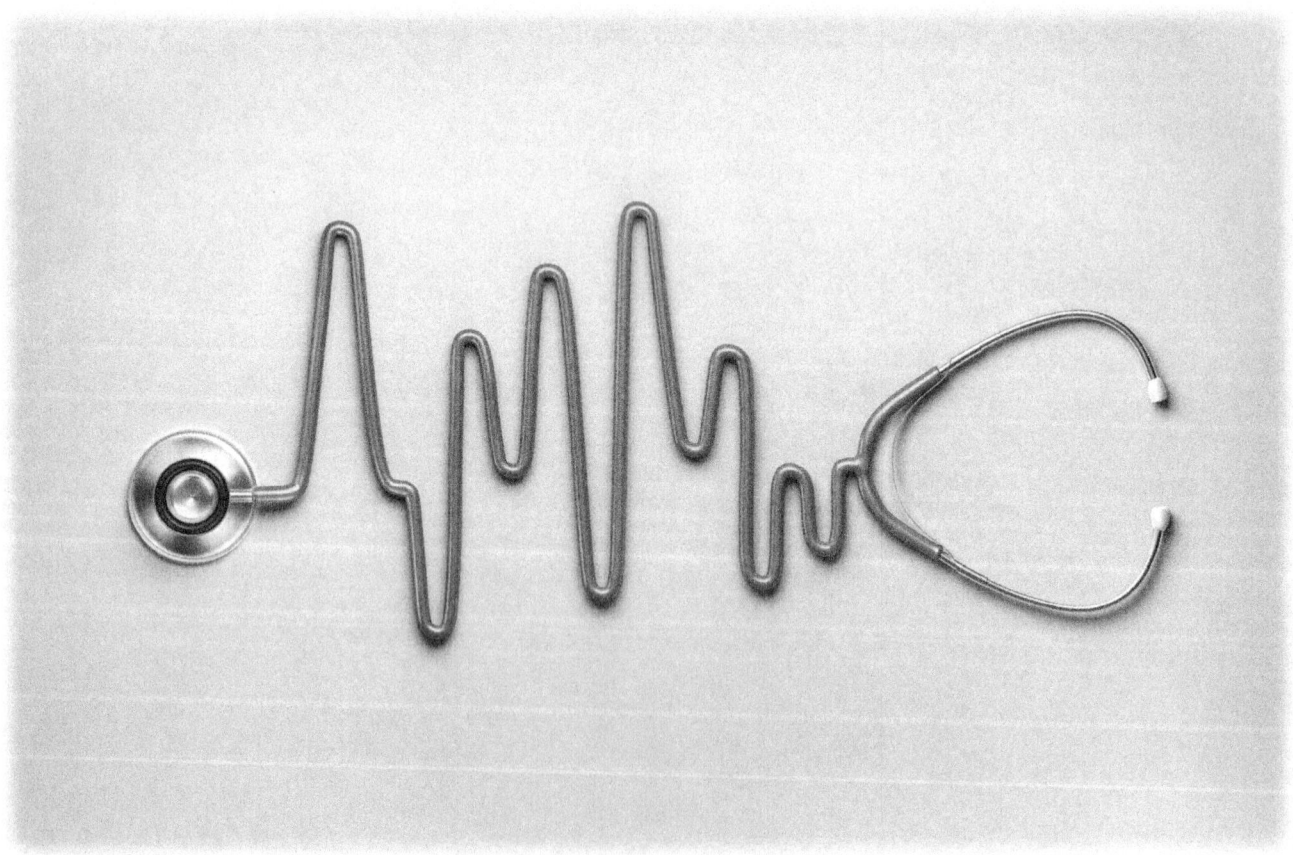

Dear Reader!

I welcome you here, on your way to forming a new habit - a healthy diet, is most beneficial for your heart! In the pages of this cookbook, you will find cholesterol-lowering recipes. You can also use the suggested 28-day meal plan with a shopping sheet to plan your diet in the future. In each recipe, you will find nutritional information to make it easier for you to understand what you are eating and to calculate your calorie intake. Each recipe has been worked out in my cookery school.

I didn't come to an understanding of healthy eating all at once. I was obese in high school and had a lot of bad diagnoses. I felt unwell, weak, and short of breath. But then divine guidance intervened, and I had to take charge of my health and appearance because of love! I completed an excellent Nutrition and dietetics courses, where I learned a lot about metabolism and was able to put everything into practice. As a result, in 2000 days of a pleasant and easy way of forming healthy habits, I lost 20kg and my tests came back to normal!

Yes, we know that cholesterol "from food" has only a 20% effect on the "internal" cholesterol that causes all the problems. But, firstly, 20% is a lot! Secondly, proper nutrition on a low-cholesterol diet involves not only reducing cholesterol but also controlling the level of carbohydrates, and calories, increasing the level of protein. The principles of healthy eating and lifestyle are in this book and will support you in forming healthy habits. It is very important to maintain a proper daily regime, get enough sleep, follow the regime of physical activity, and drink enough water.

I can do it - you can do it too! I invite you to a fascinating journey on the way to a healthy self! A lot of wonderful discoveries are waiting for you, because, besides, it is very tasty! And I will always support you and will be with you until the end of your journey! I wish you a good journey and no more than 31 inches in your waist!

With love and care, your Ariana Elizabeth Montgomery!

Table Of Contents

Starting page

Dear Reader! 3

.... 4

Table Of Contents 4

Part 1: Understanding Cholesterol and Heart Health 9

    Basics of Cholesterol and Its Impact on Health 9

    The Difference Between LDL (Bad) Cholesterol and HDL (Good) Cholesterol 9

    Cholesterol Levels and Overall Heart Health 9

    Key Ingredients for a Heart-Healthy Diet 9

    Foods to Limit or Avoid 10

Part 2: Getting Started with Heart-Healthy Habits 11

    Embracing Heart-Healthy Habits for a Vibrant Life 11

Part 3: Potential cholesterol-lowering supplements 12

    Omega-3 Fatty Acids 12

    Plant Sterols and Stanols: 12

    Psyllium: 12

    Red Yeast Rice 12

    Niacin: 12

    Coenzyme Q10 (CoQ10): 12

    Garlic: 12

    Green Tea Extract 12

    Policosanol 12

    Bergamot 12

    Soy Protein 12

Part 4: Recipes 13

    Breakfast 13

        Cottage Cheese with Fresh Pineapple 13

        Overnight Oats with Fruit 13

        Creamy Oat Banana Pancakes 14

        Avocado Toast with Black Pepper 14

        Avocado Bracket Bowl 14

        Coconut Milk Chia Pudding with Nuts and Dried Fruits 15

        Nut and Seed Granola with Almond Milk 15

        Egg White Veggie Scramble 16

        Almond Butter and Banana on Whole Grain Bread 16

        Chia Seed Pudding with Almond Milk and Mixed Berries 16

        Steel-Cut Oats with Almond Slivers and Peach Slices 17

Greek Yogurt with Honey, Walnuts, and Sliced Strawberries 17
Sweet Potato Hash with Black Beans and Avocado 17
Overnight Oats with Chia Seeds, Almond Milk, and Blueberries 18
Whole Grain Toast with Ricotta Cheese and Sliced Pears 18
Vegan Blueberry Muffins with Oat Milk and Coconut Oil 19
Quinoa Breakfast Bowl with Sliced Almonds, Banana, and Cinnamon 19
Baked Sweet Potato Filled with Black Beans, Corn, and Avocado Salsa 19
Spinach Pineapple Smoothie Bowl with Banana and Flaxseeds 20
Buckwheat Pancakes with Fresh Berries and Maple Syrup 20
Vegan Tofu Scramble with Turmeric, Bell Peppers, Onions, and Spinach 21
Baked Oatmeal Squares with Apple Slices and Pecans 21
Veggie Breakfast Tacos 22
Avocado Berry Smoothie 22
Egg White and Salmon Roll-Ups 22
Apple Cinnamon Porridge 23
Quinoa Breakfast Bowls 23
Barley and Apple Porridge 24
Tofu and Vegetable Breakfast Tacos 24
Pumpkin Spice Oatmeal 24
Zucchini Bread Oatmeal 25
Breakfast Quinoa with Apples and Walnuts 25
Sweet Potato and Kale Breakfast Hash 26
Cauliflower Rice Porridge 26
Almond and Blueberry Breakfast Smoothie 27

Appetizers, Snacks, Smoothies 27
Celery Sticks with Peanut Butter 27
Roasted Chickpeas 28
Creamy Avocado Smoothie 28
Greek Yogurt with Mixed Berries 28
Avocado Chocolate Smoothie with Almonds 29
Peanut Butter Cup Protein Shake 29
Berry Spinach Surprise: Mixed Berries, Spinach, and Chia Seeds 29
Berry Keto Smoothie with Raspberry and Coconut Milk 30
Classic Hummus with Whole-Wheat Crackers 30
Green Tea Smoothie with Mint and Lemon 30
Multigrain Berry Bar 31
Classic Guacamole 31
Peanut Butter and Banana Roll-Ups 31
Avocado Toast with Tomato Salsa 32
Cucumber Hummus Bite 32
Fruit Kabobs with Yogurt Dip 32
Spinach and Feta Stuffed Mushrooms 33
Vegetable Spring Rolls 33
Almond Berry Banana Boost 33
Cinnamon Apple Almond Smoothie 34
Blueberry Almond Antioxidant Smoothie 34
Green Almond Energizer Smoothie 34
Tropical Almond Delight Smoothie 35
Mango-Banana Green Smoothie 35
Pineapple Coconut Smoothie 35
Green Matcha Smoothie 36
Berry Beet Smoothie 36
Carrot Ginger Turmeric Smoothie 36

Salads 37
Kale and Quinoa Salad with Lemon-Tahini Dressing 37
Spinach and Berry Salad with Poppy Seed Dressing 37
Avocado and Black Bean Salad with Cilantro-Lime Dressing 37
Mixed Greens with Apple and Walnut Vinaigrette 38

Mediterranean Chickpea Salad with Herb Dressing 38
Crunchy Cabbage Slaw with Sesame Ginger Dressing 38
Roasted Beet and Goat Cheese Salad with Balsamic Reduction 39
Summer Berry Spinach Salad with Honey Lime Dressing 39
Greek Salad with Herb Marinated Olives 39
Chickpea and Quinoa Salad 39
Southwest Quinoa and Black Bean Salad with Avocado Lime Dressing 40
Mango Avocado Salad with Honey Lime Dressing 40
Tomato Basil Mozzarella Salad 40
Cucumber Tomato Salad with Cilantro and Lime 41
Arugula and Pear Salad 41
Broccoli Cranberry Salad 41
Cucumber Yogurt Salad 42
Warm Cauliflower Salad 42
Avocado Caprese Salad 43
Vegetarian Niçoise Salad 43

Soups 44

Classic Vegetable Soup 44
Butternut Squash Soup 44
Tomato Basil Soup 45
Chickpea and Spinach Soup 45
Mushroom Barley Soup 45
Creamy Potato Leek Soup 46
Creamy Broccoli and Cauliflower Soup 46
Carrot Ginger Soup 47
Golden Lentil and Spinach Soup 47
Vegetable Quinoa Soup 48
Miso Soup with Tofu and Seaweed 48
Kale and White Bean Soup 49
Spicy Black Bean Soup 49
Sweet Corn and Zucchini Soup 49
Barley and Mushroom Stew 50
Lemon Cucumber Soup with Cilantro, Olives, and Capers 50
Cabbage Soup with Beans and Tomatoes 51
White Garlic Bean Soup 51
Artichoke Soup with Spinach and Lemon 51
White Bean Puree Soup with Pumpkin and Ginger 52
Oat Soup with Vegetables and Shrimp 52
Cauliflower Soup with Broccoli and Potato 53
Chicken Broth Curry Soup with Vegetables 53
Tomato Cocktail Soup with Shrimp and Avocado 53
Onion Soup with Potato and Carrot 54

Sauces 54

Avocado Cilantro Lime Sauce 55
Basil Pesto with Walnuts 55
Peanut Ginger Sauce 55
Tomato and Roasted Red Pepper Sauce 56
Golden Turmeric Tahini Sauce 56
Mango Avocado Salsa 56
Lemon Ginger Sauce 57
Low-fat Horseradish Sauce 57
Chimichurri Sauce 57
Blueberry Lemon Sauce 58
Creamy Dill Sauce 58
Spicy Mustard Sauce 58
Roasted Garlic Sauce 59
Cucumber Dill Yogurt Sauce 59

Main course 59

Meat 59
    Oven-Roasted Turkey Breast 59
    Chicken Kebabs with Vegetables 60
    Grilled Lemon Herb Chicken Breast 60
    Baked Beef Steak with Herbs 61
    Turkey Patties with Oats 61
    Stuffed Chicken Breasts with Spinach and Mushrooms 61
    Turmeric-Ginger Baked Chicken 62
    Herb-Crusted Lamb Chops 62
    Mediterranean Turkey Burgers 63
    Rosemary Chicken and Potatoes 63
    Braised Turkey with Vegetables and Lentils 63
    Beef in its Own Juice with Zucchini and Pumpkin 64
    Grilled Chicken with Avocado Salsa 64
    Turkey Chili with Beans and Vegetables 64
    Baked Chicken Thighs with Rosemary and Garlic 65
    Beef Stir-Fry with Broccoli and Bell Peppers 65
    Roasted Chicken Quarters with Herbs and Root Vegetables 66
    Turkey Meatballs in Marinara Sauce over Zucchini Noodles 66
    Herb-Roasted Lamb Leg with Mint Yogurt Sauce 67
    Turkey Meatloaf with Zucchini 67
    Balsamic Glazed Chicken Breast 68
    Spiced Lean Pork Tenderloin 68
    Beef Stir-fry with Broccoli and Bell Pepper 68
    Chicken Zucchini Skewers 69
    Lean Beef and Vegetable Kebabs 69

Fish and Seafood 70
    Baked Salmon with Green Vegetables 70
    Steamed Fish with Lemon and Herbs 70
    Baked Tuna Carpaccio 71
    Baked Salmon with Dill and Lemon 71
    Sautéed Shrimp with Garlic and Lemon 71
    Grilled Lemon Garlic Shrimp Skewers 72
    Broiled Cod with Tomato Basil Salsa 72
    Grilled Swordfish with Mango Salsa 72
    Pan-Seared Scallops with Garlic Herb Butter 73
    Grilled Mahi Mahi with Pineapple Salsa 73
    Grilled Tuna Steaks with Mango Salsa 73
    Herb-Baked Tilapia with Lemon Quinoa 74
    Shrimp Scampi with Whole Wheat Pasta 74
    Seared Scallops with Sweet Corn Puree 75
    Grilled Salmon with Dill and Lemon 75
    Lemon Garlic Shrimp Skewers with Asparagus 75
    Baked Cod with Tomatoes, Olives, and Capers 76
    Spicy Grilled Shrimp with Yogurt Sauce 76
    Tilapia Tacos with Cabbage Slaw 77
    Herb-Crusted Halibut 77

Vegetarian Dishes 78
    Quinoa Stuffed Bell Peppers 78
    Lentil and Vegetable Stew 78
    Garlic Roasted Cauliflower Steaks 79
    Tofu and Broccoli Stir-Fry 79
    Spaghetti Squash with Marinara Sauce 79
    Black Bean and Corn Tacos 80
    Vegetarian Chili with Quinoa 80
    Zucchini Noodles with Pesto 81
    Baked Cod with Olive Tapenade 81
    Stuffed Eggplant with Lentils 82

- Lentil and Walnut Burgers ... 82
- Tofu Stir-Fry with Vegetables ... 82
- Seitan Beef Stew ... 83
- Black Bean and Sweet Potato Chili ... 83
- Tempeh Bacon BLT ... 84
- Edamame Hummus Wrap ... 84
- Vegan Meatloaf with Lentils and Mushrooms ... 85
- Soy Curl Fajitas ... 85
- Pea Protein Burgers ... 86

Desserts ... 86
- Fruit Salad with Yogurt ... 86
- Carrot and Apple Loaf ... 87
- Pear Crumble with Oat Topping ... 87
- Red Currant Jelly ... 88
- Cottage Cheese Pudding with Vanilla ... 88
- Buckwheat Pancakes with Berry Sause ... 88
- Strawberry Tiramisu Without Sugar ... 89
- Cinnamon Apple Chips ... 89
- Banana Ice Cream ... 90
- Avocado Chocolate Pudding ... 90
- Apple Cinnamon Oat Cookies ... 90
- Fresh Fruit Compote ... 91
- Raspberry Lime Sorbet ... 91
- Agar Fruit Jelly ... 91
- Pumpkin Mousse ... 92
- Berry and Flaxseed Muffins ... 92
- Steamed Apple Pies ... 93
- Almond and Coconut Biscotti ... 93
- Peach and Berry Cobbler ... 94
- Mango and Chia Seed Parfait ... 94
- Pineapple Sorbet ... 95
- Oatmeal and Raisin Cookies ... 95
- Baked Apples with Cinnamon ... 95
- Pumpkin and Spice Pudding ... 96
- Vanilla and Berry Yogurt Pops ... 96

From the writer ... 98

Meal plan ... 99

28 days ... 99

Shopping List ... 104

Part 5: Sustaining Heart-Healthy Habits ... 105
- Strategies for Sticking with Your New Eating Habits ... 105
- Adjusting Your Diet as Your Health and Nutritional Needs Change ... 105
- Incorporating Physical Activity into a Heart-Healthy Lifestyle ... 105

Appendices ... 106
- Glossary of Terms Related to Cholesterol and Heart Health ... 106
- Nutritional Information and Resources ... 107

Measurement Conversion Table ... 108

Index: ... 108

Part 1: Understanding Cholesterol and Heart Health

Basics of Cholesterol and Its Impact on Health

Cholesterol is a waxy substance found in your blood that's essential for building healthy cells. However, high levels of cholesterol can increase your risk of heart disease. Arteries can become clogged with fatty deposits, leading to atherosclerosis, which can result in heart attacks and strokes. The latest studies, such as those from the "Journal of the American College of Cardiology," have begun to challenge the traditional views on HDL, commonly known as "good cholesterol," suggesting that its role in predicting heart disease may not be as clear-cut as previously thought.

The Difference Between LDL (Bad) Cholesterol and HDL (Good) Cholesterol

LDL (low-density lipoprotein) is often referred to as "bad" cholesterol because high levels can lead to plaque buildup in arteries. Conversely, HDL (high-density lipoprotein) is considered "good" because it helps remove other forms of cholesterol from your bloodstream. Recent research, however, indicates that the protective effects of HDL may not be universal across different ethnicities, necessitating a more personalized approach to cholesterol management.

Cholesterol Levels and Overall Heart Health

Diet plays a crucial role in managing cholesterol levels. Saturated fats and trans fats increase LDL levels, while foods high in omega-3 fatty acids, soluble fiber, and plant sterols can help lower them. Dietary patterns like the Mediterranean diet, rich in fruits, vegetables, whole grains, and healthy fats, have been endorsed for their beneficial effects on cholesterol and heart health. Studies also emphasize the importance of dietary patterns over individual nutrients in managing cholesterol and reducing cardiovascular risk.

Key Ingredients for a Heart-Healthy Diet

A heart-healthy diet plays a crucial role in managing cholesterol levels and promoting overall cardiovascular health. Incorporating a variety of nutrient-rich foods into your daily meals can make a significant difference in your heart health. This chapter delves deeper into the key ingredients that form the cornerstone of a heart-healthy diet, as outlined in our cookbook, and provides guidance on how to integrate these into your meals effectively.

Fruits and Vegetables: These are fundamental to any heart-healthy diet, rich in essential nutrients, antioxidants, and dietary fiber. They help reduce the risk of heart disease by lowering blood pressure, improving vessel function, and fighting inflammation. Aim for a variety of colors on your plate to ensure a wide range of nutrients. Dark, leafy greens like spinach and kale are especially beneficial due to their high content of vitamins and minerals. Berries, apples, and citrus fruits are excellent sources of vitamin C and soluble fiber, which can aid in cholesterol management.

Whole Grains: Foods such as oats, barley, brown rice, and whole wheat contain soluble fiber, which helps reduce the absorption of cholesterol into your bloodstream. Incorporating whole grains into your diet can also help improve blood sugar levels, essential for preventing diabetes, a risk factor for heart disease. Opt for whole-grain versions of bread, pasta, and cereal to increase your intake of these healthful grains.

Healthy Fats: Not all fats are created equal. Monounsaturated and polyunsaturated fats, particularly omega-3 fatty acids found in fish like salmon, mackerel, and sardines, as well as in flaxseeds and walnuts, are known to support heart health. They can help reduce overall cholesterol levels and decrease the risk of heart disease. Cooking with olive oil, a source of monounsaturated fats, instead of butter or lard, can also contribute to a healthier heart.

Nuts and Seeds: Almonds, walnuts, flaxseeds, and chia seeds are excellent sources of monounsaturated and polyunsaturated fats, fiber, and protein. They can help maintain healthy cholesterol levels and promote heart health when consumed in moderation due to their high-calorie content. Incorporating a small handful of nuts or a tablespoon of seeds into your daily diet can provide heart-healthy benefits.

Legumes: Beans, lentils, and peas are high in soluble fiber, protein, and important nutrients like potassium, which can help lower blood pressure and cholesterol levels. They are also low in fat and a healthy alternative to meat due to their protein content. Adding legumes to soups, salads, or as a main dish can enhance the nutritional quality of your meals and support heart health.

In addition to focusing on these key ingredients, it's important to limit the intake of foods high in saturated fats, trans fats, sodium, and sugars. Reducing consumption of red meat, butter, cheese, fried foods, and sugary snacks and beverages can help manage cholesterol levels and reduce the risk of heart disease.

Foods to Limit or Avoid

Saturated Fats: Saturated fats are typically solid at room temperature and are found in various animal products and some plant oils. While they are an essential part of a balanced diet in moderation, excessive consumption of saturated fats has been linked to higher levels of LDL (low-density lipoprotein) cholesterol, which is known to increase the risk of heart disease. Foods high in saturated fats include red meats like beef and lamb, dairy products such as butter and cheese, and tropical oils like coconut oil and palm oil. When looking to limit saturated fats, opt for lean cuts of meat, low-fat dairy options, and use oils high in unsaturated fats, like olive oil, for cooking.

Trans Fats: Trans fats are created by adding hydrogen to vegetable oil through a process called hydrogenation, which makes the oil less likely to spoil. Eating foods rich in trans fats increases the amount of harmful LDL cholesterol in the bloodstream and reduces the amount of beneficial HDL cholesterol. Trans fats create inflammation, which is linked to heart disease, stroke, diabetes, and other chronic conditions. They are found in some fried foods, doughnuts, cookies, and crackers. Always check the labels for partially hydrogenated oils to avoid trans fats.

High-Sodium Foods: Sodium is a mineral that's essential for proper fluid balance in the body. However, too much sodium can lead to hypertension (high blood pressure), which is a significant risk factor for heart disease and stroke. Processed and prepared foods like canned soups, lunch meats, and fast food typically have high sodium content. To reduce sodium intake, cook at home more often, choose fresh or frozen vegetables instead of canned, and use herbs and spices instead of salt to flavor your food.

Sugary Foods and Beverages: Foods and drinks high in sugar can be very detrimental to heart health. They contribute to weight gain and can lead to obesity, which significantly increases the risk of heart disease. Furthermore, high sugar intake can lead to insulin resistance, diabetes, and increased triglyceride levels—all of which are risk factors for heart disease. Sugary foods and beverages include soda, sweets, desserts, and many breakfast cereals. Instead of sugary snacks, opt for fruits, nuts, and seeds, and choose water or unsweetened beverages over sugary drinks.

By integrating the latest research findings into this overview, the content provides readers with a contemporary and science-backed foundation for understanding cholesterol and heart health. This will set the stage for the recipes and meal plans included in the subsequent sections of the book.

Part 2: Getting Started with Heart-Healthy Habits

Embracing Heart-Healthy Habits for a Vibrant Life

Understanding Heart-Healthy Habits

Heart-healthy habits are behaviors that research has shown to reduce the risk of heart disease. These include eating balanced diets, engaging in regular physical activity, managing stress, and avoiding tobacco. Recent studies, such as those by the American Heart Association, emphasize not just what we eat, but how we live our day-to-day lives.

Creating a Heart-Healthy Environment

Your environment plays a significant role in your health journey. Start by stocking your kitchen with whole grains, fruits, vegetables, lean proteins, and healthy fats. Learn to read labels and choose items with lower levels of sodium, added sugars, and unhealthy fats. Plan your meals to include a balance of macronutrients – carbohydrates, proteins, and fats – while focusing on high-fiber foods that help lower cholesterol.

Heart-Healthy Eating Principles

Adopting heart-healthy eating principles means more than just choosing the right foods; it's about understanding portion sizes, the importance of meal timing, and how to balance your plate. Incorporate a variety of colors from fruits and vegetables to ensure a range of nutrients, and select whole grains over refined ones to maximize fiber intake.

Heart-Healthy Cooking Techniques

Healthy cooking is not just about what you cook, but how you cook it. Techniques such as grilling, broiling, steaming, and sautéing can reduce the need for added fats. Experiment with herbs and spices instead of salt to add flavor. Embrace methods that help retain the nutritional value of foods while minimizing the addition of unhealthy ingredients.

Adopting New Habits

Change doesn't happen overnight. Start small, with one or two changes at a time, such as switching to whole grains or adding an extra serving of vegetables to your meals. Use a habit tracker to monitor your progress and celebrate small victories to keep yourself motivated.

Overcoming Challenges

Facing challenges head-on is part of the journey. Whether it's budgeting for healthier food options, finding time to cook, or simply lacking motivation, each obstacle has a solution. Meal prep can save time and money, and having a support system can provide an extra push on tough days.

Physical Activity and Heart Health

Physical activity is a cornerstone of heart health. The American Heart Association recommends at least 150 minutes of moderate-intensity aerobic exercise per week. This can include brisk walking, cycling, or swimming. Remember, any movement is better than none, so find an activity you enjoy and stick with it.

Part 3: Potential cholesterol-lowering supplements

Omega-3 Fatty Acids
Omega-3 supplements, often derived from fish oil, flaxseed oil, or algae, are known for their ability to help reduce triglyceride levels. Some studies suggest they can also improve cardiovascular health by modestly lowering levels of total cholesterol and LDL cholesterol.

Plant Sterols and Stanols:
These substances, which are naturally found in small amounts in many fruits, vegetables, nuts, seeds, cereals, and other plant sources, can help reduce the absorption of cholesterol in the intestines. Many products are fortified with sterols or stanols, and they're also available as supplements.

Psyllium:
A type of fiber found in some cereal products and available as a supplement, psyllium can help lower LDL cholesterol levels. It's often found in over-the-counter laxatives and fiber supplements like Metamucil.

Red Yeast Rice
Red yeast rice contains a natural statin called monacolin K, which can help to lower LDL cholesterol. However, the amount of monacolin K can vary widely in these supplements, and there are potential side effects and interactions similar to those of prescription statins.

Niacin:
Niacin, or vitamin B3, in high doses can lower LDL cholesterol and triglycerides and raise HDL cholesterol. However, niacin supplements might have side effects and are generally not recommended for cholesterol management without medical supervision.

Coenzyme Q10 (CoQ10):
While CoQ10 is often taken to help manage side effects from statin medications, its effects on cholesterol levels are unclear. It's an antioxidant and plays a key role in metabolism.

Garlic:
Garlic supplements have been suggested to have a beneficial effect on cholesterol levels, but research results have been mixed.

Green Tea Extract
Green tea and its extract contain powerful antioxidants that may have a modest effect on lowering LDL cholesterol levels.

Policosanol
Derived from sugar cane or beeswax, policosanol was once thought to lower LDL cholesterol but recent studies have shown inconsistent results.

Bergamot
Bergamot is a type of citrus fruit whose extracts are claimed to improve several cardiovascular risk factors including lipid levels.

Soy Protein
Soy protein supplements, sometimes used as a replacement for animal protein, may have a small effect on lowering cholesterol.

It's important to note that while these supplements may contribute to cholesterol management, they should not replace medications prescribed by a healthcare provider for those with high cholesterol or other lipid disorders. Additionally, the quality of supplements can vary greatly between brands and batches, and not all supplements are thoroughly regulated.

Before beginning any supplement regimen, it's crucial to consult with a healthcare provider to discuss potential benefits, side effects, and interactions with other medications you may be taking.

Part 4: Recipes

Breakfast

Cottage Cheese with Fresh Pineapple

Yield: 4 servings | Prep Time: 10 minutes | Cook Time: 0 minutes

Ingredients:
- 2 cups low-fat cottage cheese
- 1 cup fresh pineapple, diced
- Optional: a drizzle of honey or a sprinkle of cinnamon for extra flavor

Directions:
1. Divide the cottage cheese evenly among four bowls.
2. Top each bowl with a quarter cup of diced fresh pineapple.
3. If desired, add a light drizzle of honey or a sprinkle of cinnamon for added sweetness and flavor.
4. Serve immediately or chill in the refrigerator for a cold breakfast treat.

Nutritional Information (approximate per serving):
Calories: 180kcal | Protein: 28g | Carbohydrates: 20g | Fat: 2g | Cholesterol: 10mg | Sodium: 500mg | Fiber: 1g | Potassium: 200mg

Overnight Oats with Fruit

Yield: 4 servings | Prep time: 10 minutes | Cook time: 0 minutes

Ingredients:
- 2 cups old-fashioned rolled oats
- 2 cups unsweetened almond milk
- 1/2 cup Greek yogurt
- 1 tablespoon honey or maple syrup
- 1 teaspoon vanilla extract
- 1 cup mixed fresh berries (strawberries, blueberries, raspberries)
- 1 banana, sliced
- 1/4 cup chopped nuts (such as almonds or walnuts)
- Optional toppings: additional honey or maple syrup, shredded coconut, chia seeds

Directions:
1. In a large mixing bowl, combine rolled oats, almond milk, Greek yogurt, honey (or maple syrup), and vanilla extract. Stir well to combine.
2. Gently fold in the mixed fresh berries, sliced banana, and chopped nuts.
3. Divide the mixture evenly among four Mason jars or airtight containers.
4. Cover and refrigerate overnight, or for at least 4 hours, to allow the oats to soften and flavors to meld.

5. Before serving, stir the oats and fruit mixture to combine. Add optional toppings as desired.

Nutritional Information (approximate per serving):
Calories: 275kcal | Protein: 10g | Carbohydrates: 42g | Fat: 7g | Cholesterol: 0mg | Sodium: 90mg | Fiber: 6g | Potassium: 295mg

Creamy Oat Banana Pancakes

Yield: 4 servings | Prep time: 10 minutes | Cook time: 15 minutes

Ingredients:
- 1 cup all-purpose flour
- 1/2 cup rolled oats
- 2 teaspoons baking powder
- 1/4 teaspoon salt
- 1 tablespoon sugar
- 1 large egg
- 3/4 cup milk
- 2 ripe bananas, mashed
- 1/4 cup plain Greek yogurt
- 1 teaspoon vanilla extract
- Butter or oil for cooking

Directions:
1. In a large bowl, mix together flour, rolled oats, baking powder, salt, and sugar.
2. In another bowl, beat the egg and then add milk, mashed bananas, Greek yogurt, and vanilla extract; mix well.
3. Pour the wet ingredients into the dry ingredients and stir until just combined.
4. Heat a non-stick skillet over medium heat and brush with butter or oil.
5. Pour 1/4 cup of batter for each pancake and cook until bubbles form on the surface, then flip and cook until golden brown.
6. Serve warm with your choice of toppings.

Nutritional information (approximate per serving):
 Calories: 280kcal | Protein: 9g | Carbohydrates: 52g | Fat: 4.5g | Cholesterol: 55mg | Sodium: 490mg | Fiber: 4g | Potassium: 350mg.

Avocado Toast with Black Pepper

Yield: 4 servings | Prep time: 5 minutes | Cook time: 3 minutes

Ingredients:
- 4 slices of whole-grain bread
- 2 ripe avocados
- 2 teaspoons lemon juice
- Freshly ground black pepper to taste
- Sea salt to taste
- Optional garnishes: sliced radishes, sprouts, or a drizzle of olive oil

Directions:
1. Toast the bread slices to your desired level of crispiness.
2. Halve the avocados, remove the pit, and scoop the flesh into a bowl. Add lemon juice, sea salt, and a generous amount of black pepper. Mash the ingredients together while keeping some chunks for texture.
3. Spread the mashed avocado mixture on the toasted bread slices. Add more black pepper on top if desired.
4. Garnish with optional items like sliced radishes or sprouts and a drizzle of olive oil if using.

Nutritional information (approximate per serving):
Calories: 230kcal | Protein: 5g | Carbohydrates: 26g | Fat: 12g | Cholesterol: 0mg | Sodium: 150mg | Fiber: 7g | Potassium: 487mg

Avocado Bracket Bowl

Yield: 4 servings | Prep time: 20 minutes | Cook time: 0 minutes

Ingredients:
- 2 ripe avocados, peeled and pitted
- 1 cup cooked quinoa
- 1 cup canned black beans, drained and rinsed

- 1 cup corn kernels (fresh, canned, or thawed from frozen)
- 1 cup cherry tomatoes, halved
- 1/2 red onion, finely chopped
- 1/4 cup fresh cilantro, chopped
- Juice of 1 lime
- Salt and pepper to taste
- 1 teaspoon ground cumin
- 1/4 teaspoon chili powder (optional)
- 2 tablespoons olive oil

Directions:
1. In a large bowl, combine the cooked quinoa, black beans, corn, cherry tomatoes, and red onion. Mix well.
2. In a small bowl, whisk together the lime juice, olive oil, ground cumin, chili powder (if using), salt, and pepper to create the dressing.
3. Pour the dressing over the quinoa mixture and toss until everything is evenly coated. Gently fold in the avocado chunks and cilantro.
4. Divide the mixture evenly among bowls and serve immediately or chill in the refrigerator until ready to serve.

Nutritional Information (approximate per serving):
Calories: 350 kcal | Protein: 9g | Carbohydrates: 45g | Fat: 18g | Cholesterol: 0mg | Sodium: 200mg | Fiber: 12g | Potassium: 850mg

Coconut Milk Chia Pudding with Nuts and Dried Fruits

Yield: 4 servings | Prep time: 10 minutes | Cook time: 0 minutes (Chill time: 4 hours)

Ingredients:
- 1/4 cup chia seeds
- 1 cup unsweetened coconut milk
- 1 tablespoon honey or maple syrup
- 1/2 teaspoon pure vanilla extract
- 1/4 cup mixed nuts (almonds, walnuts, pecans), roughly chopped
- 1/4 cup mixed dried fruits (raisins, apricots, dates), chopped
- Pinch of salt

Directions:
1. In a mixing bowl, whisk together the chia seeds, coconut milk, honey or maple syrup, vanilla extract, and a pinch of salt until well combined.
2. Stir in half of the chopped nuts and dried fruits, reserving the rest for topping.
3. Divide the mixture into serving glasses or bowls, cover, and refrigerate for at least 4 hours, or overnight, until the pudding has set.
4. Before serving, top the chia pudding with the remaining nuts and dried fruits.

Nutritional Information (approximate per serving):
Calories: 200 kcal | Protein: 4g | Carbohydrates: 24g | Fat: 10g | Cholesterol: 0mg | Sodium: 50mg | Fiber: 7g | Potassium: 150mg

Nut and Seed Granola with Almond Milk

Yield: 4 servings | Prep time: 10 minutes | Cook time: 20 minutes

Ingredients:
- 2 cups rolled oats
- 1/4 cup raw almonds, chopped
- 1/4 cup raw walnuts, chopped
- 1/4 cup pumpkin seeds
- 1/4 cup sunflower seeds
- 1/4 cup unsweetened shredded coconut
- 1/4 cup honey or maple syrup
- 2 tablespoons coconut oil, melted
- 1/2 teaspoon vanilla extract
- 1/2 teaspoon ground cinnamon
- A pinch of salt
- Almond milk for serving

Directions:
1. Preheat your oven to 325°F (163°C). Line a baking sheet with parchment paper.
2. In a large bowl, combine the oats, almonds, walnuts, pumpkin seeds, sunflower seeds, and shredded coconut.
3. In a separate bowl, whisk together the honey or maple syrup, melted coconut oil, vanilla extract, cinnamon, and a pinch of salt.
4. Pour the wet ingredients over the dry ingredients and mix until everything is well coated.
5. Spread the mixture evenly on the prepared baking sheet and bake for 20 minutes, stirring halfway through, until golden and crisp.
6. Let the granola cool completely on the baking sheet before serving with almond milk.

Nutritional Information (approximate per serving, granola only):
Calories: 380 kcal | Protein: 10g | Carbohydrates: 44g | Fat: 20g | Cholesterol: 0mg | Sodium: 10mg | Fiber: 6g | Potassium: 260mg

Egg White Veggie Scramble

Yield: 2 servings | Prep Time: 10 minutes | Cook Time: 8 minutes

Ingredients:
- 1 cup egg whites
- 1/2 cup diced bell peppers
- 1/2 cup chopped spinach
- 1/4 cup diced onions
- 1/4 cup sliced mushrooms
- 1 medium diced tomato
- Salt and pepper to taste
- 1 tsp olive oil

Directions:
1. Heat olive oil in a non-stick skillet over medium heat. Sauté onions, bell peppers, and mushrooms until tender.
2. Pour egg whites into the skillet. As they begin to set, gently pull the eggs across the pan with a spatula, forming large soft curds.
3. Add spinach and tomatoes and continue to cook until the egg whites are fully set.
4. Season with salt and pepper to taste and serve hot.

Nutritional Information (approximate per serving):
Calories: 150kcal | Protein: 15g | Carbohydrates: 8g | Fat: 5g | Cholesterol: 0mg | Sodium: 200mg | Fiber: 2g | Potassium: 300mg

Almond Butter and Banana on Whole Grain Bread

Yield: 2 servings | Prep time: 5 minutes | Cook time: 0 minutes

Ingredients:
- 4 slices whole grain bread
- 4 tablespoons almond butter
- 1 ripe banana, sliced

Directions:
1. Toast the whole grain bread slices until golden brown.
2. Spread 2 tablespoons of almond butter evenly on each slice of toast.
3. Arrange banana slices on top of the almond butter.
4. Place another slice of toast on each to make a sandwich. Cut in half if desired.

Nutritional Information (approximate per serving):
Calories: 320kcal | Protein: 11g | Carbohydrates: 39g | Fat: 15g | Cholesterol: 0mg | Sodium: 320mg | Fiber: 8g | Potassium: 450mg

Chia Seed Pudding with Almond Milk and Mixed Berries

Yield: 4 servings | Prep time: 5 minutes | Cook time: 0 minutes

Ingredients:
- 1/2 cup chia seeds
- 2 cups almond milk
- 1 teaspoon vanilla extract
- 2 tablespoons maple syrup (optional)
- 1 cup mixed berries (such as strawberries, blueberries, raspberries)

Directions:
1. In a mixing bowl, combine chia seeds, almond milk, vanilla extract, and maple syrup (if using). Stir well to combine.
2. Cover the bowl and refrigerate for at least 2 hours or overnight, allowing the chia seeds to absorb the liquid and thicken.
3. Once the chia pudding has thickened, give it a good stir to break up any clumps.
4. Divide the pudding into serving bowls or jars and top with mixed berries before serving.

Nutritional Information (approximate per serving):
Calories: 180kcal | Protein: 5g | Carbohydrates: 19g | Fat: 10g | Cholesterol: 0mg | Sodium: 80mg | Fiber: 10g | Potassium: 180mg

Steel-Cut Oats with Almond Slivers and Peach Slices

Yield: 4 servings | Prep time: 5 minutes | Cook time: 20 minutes

Ingredients:
- 1 cup steel-cut oats
- 3 cups water
- 1/4 teaspoon salt
- 1/4 cup almond slivers
- 2 ripe peaches, sliced

Directions:
1. In a medium saucepan, bring the water to a boil. Stir in the steel-cut oats and salt.
2. Reduce the heat to low and simmer, uncovered, stirring occasionally, for about 20 minutes or until the oats are tender and creamy.
3. While the oats are cooking, toast the almond slivers in a dry skillet over medium heat until golden brown and fragrant, about 3-5 minutes.
4. Once the oats are cooked, divide them into serving bowls and top with toasted almond slivers and sliced peaches.

Nutritional Information (approximate per serving):
Calories: 220kcal | Protein: 7g | Carbohydrates: 36g | Fat: 6g | Cholesterol: 0mg | Sodium: 150mg | Fiber: 6g | Potassium: 310mg

Greek Yogurt with Honey, Walnuts, and Sliced Strawberries

Yield: 2 servings | Prep time: 5 minutes | Cook time: 0 minutes

Ingredients:
- 1 cup Greek yogurt
- 2 tablespoons honey
- 1/4 cup walnuts, chopped
- 1 cup sliced strawberries

Directions:
1. Divide the Greek yogurt evenly between two serving bowls.
2. Drizzle 1 tablespoon of honey over each portion of yogurt.
3. Sprinkle chopped walnuts over the yogurt.
4. Top with sliced strawberries and serve.

Nutritional Information (approximate per serving):
Calories: 280kcal | Protein: 16g | Carbohydrates: 30g | Fat: 12g | Cholesterol: 10mg | Sodium: 50mg | Fiber: 4g | Potassium: 340mg

Sweet Potato Hash with Black Beans and Avocado

Yield: 4 servings | Prep time: 10 minutes | Cook time: 20 minutes

Ingredients:
- 2 large sweet potatoes, peeled and diced
- 1 tablespoon olive oil
- 1 small onion, diced
- 1 red bell pepper, diced
- 1 teaspoon cumin
- 1 teaspoon chili powder
- Salt and pepper to taste
- 1 can (15 oz) black beans, drained and rinsed
- 1 avocado, diced
- Optional toppings: chopped cilantro, lime wedges

Directions:
1. In a large skillet, heat olive oil over medium heat. Add diced sweet potatoes and cook for about 10 minutes, stirring occasionally, until they are tender.
2. Add diced onion and red bell pepper to the skillet with sweet potatoes. Cook for another 5-7 minutes until the vegetables are softened.
3. Sprinkle cumin, chili powder, salt, and pepper over the vegetables and stir to combine.
4. Add drained black beans to the skillet and cook for an additional 2-3 minutes until heated through.
5. Serve the sweet potato hash hot, topped with diced avocado and any optional toppings of your choice.

Nutritional Information (approximate per serving):
Calories: 320kcal | Protein: 8g | Carbohydrates: 48g | Fat: 12g | Cholesterol: 0mg | Sodium: 250mg | Fiber: 12g | Potassium: 980mg

Overnight Oats with Chia Seeds, Almond Milk, and Blueberries

Yield: 4 servings | Prep time: 5 minutes | Cook time: 0 minutes

Ingredients:
- 1 cup old-fashioned oats
- 2 tablespoons chia seeds
- 2 cups almond milk
- 1 cup blueberries (fresh or frozen)
- Optional toppings: honey, sliced almonds, additional blueberries

Directions:
1. In a large mixing bowl, combine the old-fashioned oats, chia seeds, and almond milk. Stir well to combine.
2. Gently fold in the blueberries.
3. Divide the mixture into four individual jars or containers with lids.
4. Cover and refrigerate overnight, or for at least 4 hours, to allow the oats and chia seeds to absorb the liquid and soften.
5. Before serving, stir the overnight oats and top with optional toppings if desired.

Nutritional Information (approximate per serving):
Calories: 210kcal | Protein: 6g | Carbohydrates: 34g | Fat: 6g | Cholesterol: 0mg | Sodium: 120mg | Fiber: 8g | Potassium: 250mg

Whole Grain Toast with Ricotta Cheese and Sliced Pears

Yield: 2 servings | Prep time: 5 minutes | Cook time: 5 minutes

Ingredients:
- 4 slices whole grain bread
- 1/2 cup ricotta cheese
- 1 ripe pear, thinly sliced

Directions:
1. Toast the whole grain bread slices until golden brown.
2. Spread an equal amount of ricotta cheese on each slice of toast.
3. Arrange the sliced pears on top of the ricotta cheese.
4. Serve immediately and enjoy!

Nutritional Information (approximate per serving):
Calories: 250kcal | Protein: 11g | Carbohydrates: 37g | Fat: 6g | Cholesterol: 20mg | Sodium: 300mg | Fiber: 6g | Potassium: 280mg

Vegan Blueberry Muffins with Oat Milk and Coconut Oil

Yield: 6 servings | Prep time: 10 minutes | Cook time: 20 minutes

Ingredients:
- 1 1/2 cups all-purpose flour
- 1/2 cup granulated sugar
- 2 teaspoons baking powder
- 1/2 teaspoon salt
- 3/4 cup oat milk
- 1/4 cup coconut oil, melted
- 1 teaspoon vanilla extract
- 1 cup fresh or frozen blueberries

Directions:
1. Preheat the oven to 375°F (190°C). Line a muffin tin with paper liners or grease with coconut oil.
2. In a large bowl, whisk together the flour, sugar, baking powder, and salt.
3. In a separate bowl, mix the oat milk, melted coconut oil, and vanilla extract.
4. Pour the wet ingredients into the dry ingredients and stir until just combined. Gently fold in the blueberries.
5. Divide the batter evenly among the muffin cups, filling each about 2/3 full.
6. Bake for 18-20 minutes, or until a toothpick inserted into the center of a muffin comes out clean.
7. Allow the muffins to cool in the pan for 5 minutes, then transfer to a wire rack to cool completely.

Nutritional information (approximate per serving):
Calories: 236kcal | Protein: 3g | Carbohydrates: 37g | Fat: 9g | Cholesterol: 0mg | Sodium: 299mg | Fiber: 1g | Potassium: 78mg

Quinoa Breakfast Bowl with Sliced Almonds, Banana, and Cinnamon

Yield: 2 servings | Prep time: 5 minutes | Cook time: 20 minutes

Ingredients:
- 1/2 cup quinoa
- 1 cup water
- 1 banana, sliced
- 1/4 cup sliced almonds
- 1/2 teaspoon ground cinnamon

Directions:
1. Rinse the quinoa under cold water until the water runs clear.
2. In a saucepan, bring the water to a boil. Add the rinsed quinoa, reduce heat to low, cover, and simmer for about 15 minutes, or until the water is absorbed and the quinoa is fluffy.
3. Divide the cooked quinoa between two bowls.
4. Top each bowl with sliced banana and sliced almonds.
5. Sprinkle ground cinnamon over the bowls.
6. Serve warm and enjoy!

Nutritional information (approximate per serving):
Calories: 284kcal | Protein: 9g | Carbohydrates: 45g | Fat: 8g | Cholesterol: 0mg | Sodium: 5mg | Fiber: 6g | Potassium: 451mg

Baked Sweet Potato Filled with Black Beans, Corn, and Avocado Salsa

Yield: 4 servings | Prep time: 10 minutes | Cook time: 45 minutes

Ingredients:
- 4 medium sweet potatoes
- 1 can (15 ounces) black beans, drained and rinsed
- 1 cup corn kernels (fresh, canned, or frozen)
- 1 avocado, diced
- 1/4 cup diced red onion

- 1/4 cup chopped cilantro
- Juice of 1 lime
- Salt and pepper to taste

Directions:
1. Preheat the oven to 400°F (200°C).
2. Scrub the sweet potatoes clean and pierce them several times with a fork. Place them on a baking sheet lined with parchment paper and bake for 40-45 minutes, or until tender.
3. While the sweet potatoes are baking, prepare the filling. In a large bowl, combine the black beans, corn, diced avocado, red onion, chopped cilantro, lime juice, salt, and pepper. Mix well.
4. Once the sweet potatoes are done baking, remove them from the oven and let them cool slightly.
5. Slice each sweet potato lengthwise and fluff the flesh with a fork. Spoon the black bean and corn mixture generously onto each sweet potato.
6. Serve immediately, garnished with additional cilantro and lime wedges if desired.

Nutritional information (approximate per serving):
Calories: 348kcal | Protein: 10g | Carbohydrates: 64g | Fat: 8g | Cholesterol: 0mg | Sodium: 48mg | Fiber: 14g | Potassium: 1031mg

Spinach Pineapple Smoothie Bowl with Banana and Flaxseeds

Yield: 2 servings | Prep time: 5 minutes | Cook time: 0 minutes

Ingredients:
- 2 cups fresh spinach leaves
- 1 cup frozen pineapple chunks
- 1 ripe banana
- 2 tablespoons ground flaxseeds
- 1/2 cup water or coconut water (optional for desired consistency)
- Toppings (optional): sliced banana, fresh berries, granola, coconut flakes

Directions:
1. In a blender, combine the spinach, frozen pineapple chunks, banana, flaxseeds, and water (if using).
2. Blend until smooth and creamy, adding more water as needed to reach your desired consistency.
3. Pour the smoothie into bowls.
4. Top with your favorite toppings, such as sliced banana, fresh berries, granola, or coconut flakes.
5. Serve immediately and enjoy!

Nutritional information (approximate per serving):
Calories: 214kcal | Protein: 5g | Carbohydrates: 42g | Fat: 5g | Cholesterol: 0mg | Sodium: 48mg | Fiber: 9g | Potassium: 678mg

Buckwheat Pancakes with Fresh Berries and Maple Syrup

Yield: 4 servings | Prep time: 10 minutes | Cook time: 15 minutes

Ingredients:
- 1 cup buckwheat flour
- 1 tablespoon baking powder
- 1/4 teaspoon salt
- 1 tablespoon maple syrup
- 1 cup almond milk (or any milk of your choice)
- 1 tablespoon coconut oil, melted (plus more for cooking)
- Fresh berries for topping
- Maple syrup for serving

Directions:
1. In a large bowl, whisk together the buckwheat flour, baking powder, and salt.
2. In a separate bowl, mix the maple syrup, almond milk, and melted coconut oil.
3. Pour the wet ingredients into the dry ingredients and stir until just combined. Be careful not to overmix; a few lumps are okay.
4. Heat a skillet or griddle over medium heat and lightly grease with coconut oil.

5. Pour about 1/4 cup of batter onto the skillet for each pancake. Cook until bubbles form on the surface, then flip and cook until golden brown on the other side.
6. Repeat with the remaining batter.
7. Serve the pancakes topped with fresh berries and maple syrup.

Nutritional information (approximate per serving):
Calories: 235kcal | Protein: 5g | Carbohydrates: 42g | Fat: 6g | Cholesterol: 0mg | Sodium: 366mg | Fiber: 5g | Potassium: 319mg

Vegan Tofu Scramble with Turmeric, Bell Peppers, Onions, and Spinach

Yield: 4 servings | Prep time: 10 minutes | Cook time: 15 minutes

Ingredients:
- 1 block (14 ounces) firm tofu, drained and crumbled
- 1 tablespoon olive oil
- 1/2 teaspoon turmeric powder
- 1 bell pepper, diced
- 1 small onion, diced
- 2 cups fresh spinach leaves
- Salt and pepper to taste

Directions:
1. Heat the olive oil in a large skillet over medium heat.
2. Add the diced bell pepper and onion to the skillet and sauté until softened, about 5 minutes.
3. Add the crumbled tofu and turmeric powder to the skillet. Cook, stirring occasionally, for about 5-7 minutes, until the tofu is heated through and slightly golden.
4. Stir in the fresh spinach leaves and cook for another 2-3 minutes, until the spinach is wilted.
5. Season with salt and pepper to taste.
6. Serve the tofu scramble hot, optionally with toast or avocado on the side.

Nutritional information (approximate per serving):
Calories: 146kcal | Protein: 10g | Carbohydrates: 7g | Fat: 9g | Cholesterol: 0mg | Sodium: 144mg | Fiber: 2g | Potassium: 376mg

Baked Oatmeal Squares with Apple Slices and Pecans

Yield: 6 servings | Prep time: 10 minutes | Cook time: 30 minutes

Ingredients:
- 2 cups old-fashioned rolled oats
- 1 teaspoon baking powder
- 1/2 teaspoon ground cinnamon
- 1/4 teaspoon salt
- 1 1/2 cups almond milk (or any milk of your choice)
- 1/4 cup maple syrup
- 1 large egg
- 1 teaspoon vanilla extract
- 1 apple, thinly sliced
- 1/4 cup chopped pecans

Directions:
1. Preheat the oven to 350°F (175°C). Grease or line an 8x8-inch baking dish with parchment paper.
2. In a large bowl, mix the oats, baking powder, cinnamon, and salt.
3. In another bowl, whisk together the almond milk, maple syrup, egg, and vanilla extract.
4. Pour the wet ingredients into the dry ingredients and stir until well combined.
5. Pour the mixture into the prepared baking dish. Arrange the apple slices on top and sprinkle with chopped pecans.
6. Bake for 25-30 minutes, or until the edges are golden brown and the center is set.
7. Allow to cool slightly before cutting into squares and serving.

Nutritional information (approximate per serving):
Calories: 214kcal | Protein: 5g | Carbohydrates: 34g | Fat: 7g | Cholesterol: 31mg | Sodium: 157mg | Fiber: 4g | Potassium: 199mg

Veggie Breakfast Tacos

Yield: 4 servings | Prep time: 15 minutes | Cook time: 15 minutes

Ingredients:
- 8 small corn tortillas
- 1 tablespoon olive oil
- 1 small onion, diced
- 1 bell pepper, diced
- 1 cup diced tomatoes
- 1 cup black beans, drained and rinsed
- 1 teaspoon ground cumin
- Salt and pepper to taste
- 1 avocado, sliced
- Fresh cilantro, for garnish
- Lime wedges, for serving

Directions:
1. Heat olive oil in a skillet over medium heat. Add diced onion and bell pepper, and sauté until softened, about 5 minutes.
2. Stir in diced tomatoes, black beans, ground cumin, salt, and pepper. Cook for another 5 minutes, until heated through.
3. Meanwhile, warm the corn tortillas in a separate skillet or in the microwave.
4. Assemble the tacos by spooning the veggie mixture onto the warmed tortillas. Top with avocado slices and fresh cilantro. Serve with lime wedges on the side.

Nutritional Information (approximate per serving):
Calories: 280kcal | Protein: 8g | Carbohydrates: 38g | Fat: 11g | Cholesterol: 0mg | Sodium: 310mg | Fiber: 9g | Potassium: 550mg

Avocado Berry Smoothie

Yield: 2 servings | Prep time: 5 minutes | Cook time: 0 minutes

Ingredients:
- 1 ripe avocado, peeled and pitted
- 1 cup mixed berries (such as strawberries, blueberries, raspberries)
- 1 banana, peeled
- 1 cup spinach leaves
- 1 cup almond milk (or any milk of your choice)
- 1 tablespoon honey or maple syrup (optional, for sweetness)
- Ice cubes (optional, for a colder smoothie)

Directions:
1. Place all ingredients into a blender.
2. Blend until smooth and creamy, adding more almond milk if needed to reach your desired consistency.
3. Taste and adjust sweetness by adding honey or maple syrup if desired.
4. Pour into glasses and serve immediately.

Nutritional Information (approximate per serving):
Calories: 210kcal | Protein: 4g | Carbohydrates: 26g | Fat: 12g | Cholesterol: 0mg | Sodium: 140mg | Fiber: 9g | Potassium: 630mg

Egg White and Salmon Roll-Ups

Yield: 4 servings | Prep time: 10 minutes | Cook time: 10 minutes

Ingredients:
- 8 egg whites
- 4 oz smoked salmon slices
- 1/4 cup chopped red onion
- 1/4 cup chopped fresh dill
- Salt and pepper to taste
- Cooking spray or olive oil, for greasing

Directions:
1. In a bowl, whisk together the egg whites until frothy. Season with salt and pepper.
2. Heat a non-stick skillet over medium heat and lightly grease it with cooking spray or olive oil.

3. Pour the egg whites into the skillet and swirl to create a thin layer.
4. Cook for 2-3 minutes until the edges start to set, then carefully flip and cook for another 2-3 minutes until cooked through.
5. Remove the cooked egg white sheet from the skillet and place it on a cutting board. Repeat with the remaining egg whites.
6. Once all the egg white sheets are cooked, place a slice of smoked salmon on each sheet and sprinkle with chopped red onion and fresh dill.
7. Roll up the egg white sheets tightly and slice each roll into bite-sized pieces.
8. Serve immediately or refrigerate for later.

Nutritional Information (approximate per serving):
Calories: 90kcal | Protein: 15g | Carbohydrates: 1g | Fat: 2g | Cholesterol: 5mg | Sodium: 280mg | Fiber: 0g | Potassium: 180mg.

Apple Cinnamon Porridge

Yield: 4 servings | Prep time: 5 minutes | Cook time: 15 minutes

Ingredients:
- 1 cup old-fashioned oats
- 2 cups water
- 1 cup unsweetened almond milk (or any milk of your choice)
- 2 apples, peeled, cored, and diced
- 1 tablespoon maple syrup (optional)
- 1 teaspoon ground cinnamon
- Pinch of salt
- Chopped nuts or seeds for topping (optional)

Directions:
1. In a saucepan, bring the water to a boil. Stir in the oats and reduce heat to low. Simmer for about 5 minutes, stirring occasionally, until the oats start to thicken.
2. Add the diced apples, almond milk, maple syrup (if using), cinnamon, and a pinch of salt to the saucepan. Stir well to combine.
3. Continue to cook the porridge for another 5-7 minutes, or until the apples are tender and the porridge reaches your desired consistency, stirring occasionally.
4. Once the porridge is cooked, remove from heat and let it sit for a minute to thicken.
5. Serve the porridge hot, topped with chopped nuts or seeds if desired.

Nutritional Information (approximate per serving):
Calories: 200kcal | Protein: 5g | Carbohydrates: 38g | Fat: 4g | Cholesterol: 0mg | Sodium: 80mg | Fiber: 6g | Potassium: 260mg

Quinoa Breakfast Bowls

Yield: 4 servings | Prep time: 10 minutes | Cook time: 15 minutes

Ingredients:
- 1 cup quinoa
- 2 cups water or vegetable broth
- 1 tablespoon coconut oil or butter
- 1 cup diced fresh fruit (such as berries, banana, or apple)
- 1/4 cup chopped nuts or seeds (such as almonds, walnuts, or pumpkin seeds)
- 1 tablespoon honey or maple syrup (optional)
- Ground cinnamon, to taste
- Greek yogurt or almond milk, for serving

Directions:
1. Rinse the quinoa under cold water using a fine mesh strainer.
2. In a medium saucepan, bring the water or vegetable broth to a boil. Add the rinsed quinoa and reduce heat to low. Cover and simmer for 12-15 minutes, or until all the liquid is absorbed and the quinoa is tender.
3. Fluff the cooked quinoa with a fork and stir in the coconut oil or butter until melted.
4. Divide the cooked quinoa into bowls. Top each bowl with diced fresh fruit, chopped nuts or seeds, a drizzle of honey or maple syrup (if using), and a sprinkle of ground cinnamon.

5. Serve the quinoa breakfast bowls with Greek yogurt or almond milk on the side.

Nutritional Information (approximate per serving):
Calories: 300kcal | Protein: 9g | Carbohydrates: 45g | Fat: 10g | Cholesterol: 0mg | Sodium: 10mg | Fiber: 6g | Potassium: 350mg

Barley and Apple Porridge

Yield: 4 servings | Prep time: 10 minutes | Cook time: 10 minutes

Ingredients:
- 1 cup barley
- 2 cups water
- 2 cups milk (or any plant-based milk for a vegan option)
- 2 apples, peeled, cored, and chopped
- 2 tablespoons honey or maple syrup
- 1 teaspoon cinnamon
- Pinch of salt
- Optional toppings: chopped nuts, dried fruits, additional honey or maple syrup

Directions:

1. In a saucepan, bring water to a boil. Add barley, reduce heat to low, cover, and simmer for about 15-20 minutes until barley is tender and water is absorbed.
2. Stir in milk, chopped apples, honey or maple syrup, cinnamon, and salt. Cook uncovered for another 5-7 minutes until the mixture thickens, stirring occasionally.
3. Remove from heat and let it rest for a couple of minutes. Serve hot with optional toppings if desired.

Nutritional Information (approximate per serving):
Calories: 270-540kcal | Protein: 7-14g | Carbohydrates: 54-108g | Fat: 2-4g | Cholesterol: 2-4mg | Sodium: 80-160mg | Fiber: 7-14g | Potassium: 400-800mg

Tofu and Vegetable Breakfast Tacos

Yield: 2-6 servings | Prep time: 15minutes | Cook time: 15 minutes

Ingredients:
- 8 small corn tortillas
- 1 block (about 14 oz) firm tofu, drained and crumbled
- 1 bell pepper, diced
- 1 small onion, diced
- 1 cup cherry tomatoes, halved
- 2 cloves garlic, minced
- 1 tablespoon olive oil
- 1 teaspoon ground cumin
- 1 teaspoon chili powder
- Salt and pepper to taste
- Optional toppings: avocado slices, salsa, cilantro, hot sauce

Directions:
1. Heat olive oil in a skillet over medium heat. Add diced onion and bell pepper, sauté until softened, about 5 minutes.
2. Add minced garlic and crumbled tofu to the skillet. Stir in ground cumin, chili powder, salt, and pepper. Cook for another 5-7 minutes until tofu is heated through and slightly browned.
3. Stir in cherry tomatoes and cook for an additional 2-3 minutes until tomatoes are softened.
4. Warm the corn tortillas in a separate skillet or in the microwave.
5. Assemble tacos by spooning tofu and vegetable mixture onto warmed tortillas. Add optional toppings if desired.

Nutritional Information (approximate per serving):
Calories: 230-460kcal | Protein: 12-24g | Carbohydrates: 30-60g | Fat: 7-14g | Cholesterol: 0mg | Sodium: 250-500mg | Fiber: 5-10g | Potassium: 450-900mg

Pumpkin Spice Oatmeal

Yield: 4 servings | Prep time: 5 minutes | Cook time: 10 minutes

Ingredients:
- 1 cup rolled oats
- 2 cups water or milk (dairy or plant-based)
- 1/2 cup pumpkin puree
- 2 tablespoons maple syrup or brown sugar
- 1 teaspoon pumpkin pie spice (or a mixture of cinnamon, nutmeg, ginger, and cloves)
- Pinch of salt
- Optional toppings: chopped nuts, dried cranberries, a drizzle of honey or maple syrup, a dollop of yogurt

Directions:
1. In a saucepan, bring water or milk to a boil over medium heat.
2. Stir in rolled oats, pumpkin puree, maple syrup or brown sugar, pumpkin pie spice, and a pinch of salt.
3. Reduce heat to low and simmer for about 5-7 minutes, stirring occasionally, until oatmeal is thickened and creamy.
4. Remove from heat and let it sit for a minute to cool slightly and thicken further.
5. Serve hot with optional toppings if desired.

Nutritional Information (approximate per serving):
Calories: 150-300kcal | Protein: 4-8g | Carbohydrates: 28-56g | Fat: 2-4g | Cholesterol: 0mg | Sodium: 50-100mg | Fiber: 4-8g | Potassium: 200-400mg

Zucchini Bread Oatmeal

Yield: 4 servings | Prep time: 10 minutes | Cook time: 15 minutes

Ingredients:
- 1 cup rolled oats
- 2 cups milk (dairy or plant-based)
- 1 cup grated zucchini
- 2 tablespoons maple syrup or honey
- 1 teaspoon ground cinnamon
- 1/4 teaspoon ground nutmeg
- 1/4 cup chopped walnuts or pecans (optional)
- Pinch of salt
- Optional toppings: additional maple syrup or honey, sliced bananas, dried cranberries

Directions:
1. In a saucepan, combine rolled oats and milk. Bring to a simmer over medium heat.
2. Stir in grated zucchini, maple syrup or honey, cinnamon, nutmeg, chopped nuts (if using), and a pinch of salt.
3. Cook for about 10-12 minutes, stirring occasionally, until the oats are cooked and the mixture has thickened to your desired consistency.
4. Remove from heat and let it cool for a minute before serving.
5. Serve hot with optional toppings if desired.

Nutritional Information (approximate per serving):
Calories: 160-480kcal | Protein: 6-18g | Carbohydrates: 26-78g | Fat: 3-9g | Cholesterol: 0-10mg | Sodium: 70-210mg | Fiber: 3-9g | Potassium: 260-780mg

Breakfast Quinoa with Apples and Walnuts

Yield: 4 servings | Prep time: 5 minutes | Cook time: 20 minutes

Ingredients:
- 1 cup quinoa
- 2 cups water or milk (dairy or plant-based)
- 2 apples, diced
- 1/4 cup chopped walnuts
- 2 tablespoons maple syrup or honey
- 1 teaspoon ground cinnamon
- Pinch of salt
- Optional toppings: additional maple syrup or honey, Greek yogurt, raisins

Directions:
1. Rinse quinoa under cold water using a fine mesh sieve.
2. In a saucepan, combine quinoa and water or milk. Bring to a boil, then reduce heat to low, cover, and simmer for about 15 minutes until quinoa is tender and liquid is absorbed.

3. Stir in diced apples, chopped walnuts, maple syrup or honey, cinnamon, and a pinch of salt. Cook for an additional 3-5 minutes until apples are softened and mixture is heated through.
4. Remove from heat and let it sit for a minute to cool slightly.
5. Serve hot with optional toppings if desired.

Nutritional Information (approximate per serving):
Calories: 240-720kcal | Protein: 6-18g | Carbohydrates: 40-120g | Fat: 6-18g | Cholesterol: 0-5mg | Sodium: 10-30mg | Fiber: 6-18g | Potassium: 380-1140mg

Sweet Potato and Kale Breakfast Hash

Yield: 4 servings | Prep time: 10 minutes | Cook time: 20 minutes

Ingredients:
- 2 medium sweet potatoes, peeled and diced
- 2 cups chopped kale
- 1 onion, diced
- 2 cloves garlic, minced
- 2 tablespoons olive oil
- Salt and pepper to taste
- Optional toppings: fried or poached eggs, avocado slices, hot sauce

Directions:
1. Heat olive oil in a large skillet over medium heat. Add diced sweet potatoes and cook for about 8-10 minutes, stirring occasionally, until potatoes are tender and lightly browned.
2. Add diced onion and minced garlic to the skillet. Cook for another 2-3 minutes until onion is translucent and garlic is fragrant.
3. Stir in chopped kale and cook for an additional 3-5 minutes until kale is wilted and tender.
4. Season with salt and pepper to taste.
5. Serve hot as is or with optional toppings such as fried or poached eggs, avocado slices, or hot sauce.

Nutritional Information (approximate):
Calories: 160-480kcal | Protein: 3-9g | Carbohydrates: 20-60g | Fat: 7-21g | Cholesterol: 0mg | Sodium: 60-180mg | Fiber: 3-9g | Potassium: 600-1800mg

Cauliflower Rice Porridge

Yield: 4 servings | Prep time: 10 minutes | Cook time: 15 minutes

Ingredients:
- 1 medium head cauliflower, riced (or about 4 cups store-bought cauliflower rice)
- 2 cups milk (dairy or plant-based)
- 1/2 teaspoon ground cinnamon
- 1/4 teaspoon ground nutmeg
- 2 tablespoons maple syrup or honey
- 1/4 cup chopped nuts (such as almonds, walnuts, or pecans)
- Pinch of salt
- Optional toppings: fresh berries, sliced bananas, a drizzle of maple syrup or honey

Directions:
1. In a saucepan, combine cauliflower rice and milk. Bring to a simmer over medium heat.
2. Stir in ground cinnamon, ground nutmeg, maple syrup or honey, chopped nuts, and a pinch of salt.
3. Cook for about 10-12 minutes, stirring occasionally, until cauliflower rice is tender and mixture has thickened to your desired consistency.
4. Remove from heat and let it cool for a minute before serving.
5. Serve hot with optional toppings if desired.

Nutritional Information (approximate per serving):
Calories: 80-240kcal | Protein: 3-9g | Carbohydrates: 12-36g | Fat: 2-6g | Cholesterol: 0-5mg | Sodium: 70-210mg | Fiber: 3-9g | Potassium: 300-900mg

Almond and Blueberry Breakfast Smoothie

Yield: 4 servings | Prep time: 5 minutes | Cook time: 0 minutes

Ingredients:
- 2 cups almond milk (or any milk of your choice)
- 2 cups frozen blueberries
- 1 banana
- 1/4 cup almond butter
- 1 tablespoon honey or maple syrup
- Optional: a handful of spinach or kale for added nutrition

Directions:
1. Combine all ingredients in a blender.
2. Blend until smooth and creamy, adding more almond milk if necessary to reach desired consistency.
3. Taste and adjust sweetness if needed by adding more honey or maple syrup.
4. Pour into glasses and serve immediately.

Nutritional Information (approximate per serving):
Calories: 180-540kcal | Protein: 4-12g | Carbohydrates: 25-75g | Fat: 7-21g | Cholesterol: 0mg | Sodium: 100-300mg | Fiber: 5-15g | Potassium: 400-1200mg

Appetizers, Snacks, Smoothies

Celery Sticks with Peanut Butter

Yield: 4 servings | Prep time: 5 minutes | Cook time: 0 minutes.

Ingredients:
- 8 large celery stalks
- 1/2 cup smooth or crunchy peanut butter

Directions:
1. Rinse the celery stalks and pat them dry. Trim the ends and cut each stalk into 3-4-inch-long pieces.
2. Spoon or pipe about 1 tablespoon of peanut butter
into the groove of each celery stick.
3. Arrange the celery sticks on a platter and serve as a snack or appetizer.

Nutritional Information (approximate per serving):
Calories: 160 kcal | Protein: 7g | Carbohydrates: 8g | Fat: 12g | Cholesterol: 0mg | Sodium: 150mg | Fibber: 3g | Potassium: 200mg

Roasted Chickpeas

Yield: 4 servings | Prep time: 10 minutes | Cook time: 30 minutes

Ingredients:
- 2 cans (15 ounces each) chickpeas, drained and rinsed
- 2 tablespoons olive oil
- 1/2 teaspoon salt
- 1/4 teaspoon ground black pepper
- 1/2 teaspoon paprika
- 1/4 teaspoon garlic powder
- 1/4 teaspoon onion powder
- 1/4 teaspoon ground cumin

Directions:
1. Preheat oven to 400°F (204°C). Pat the chickpeas dry with paper towels and remove any loose skins.
2. In a bowl, toss the chickpeas with olive oil, salt, pepper, paprika, garlic powder, onion powder, and cumin until evenly coated.
3. Spread the chickpeas out in an even layer on a baking sheet.
4. Roast in the preheated oven for 25-30 minutes, stirring or shaking the pan halfway through, until the chickpeas are golden and crispy.
5. Remove from the oven and let cool slightly before serving. They will continue to crisp up as they cool.

Nutritional Information (approximate per serving):
Calories: 210 kcal | Protein: 10g | Carbohydrates: 35g | Fat: 4g | Cholesterol: 0mg | Sodium: 300mg | Fiber: 10g | Potassium: 320mg

Creamy Avocado Smoothie

Yield: 2 servings | Prep time: 5 minutes | Cook time: 0 minutes

Ingredients:
- 1 ripe avocado
- 1 banana
- 1 cup spinach leaves
- 1 cup unsweetened almond milk
- 1/2 cup plain Greek yogurt
- 1 tablespoon honey (or to taste)
- 1/2 cup ice cubes
- Optional: 1 tablespoon chia seeds for extra fiber and nutrients

Directions:
1. Cut the avocado in half, remove the pit, and scoop the flesh into a blender.
2. Add the banana, spinach, almond milk, Greek yogurt, honey, and ice cubes to the blender.
3. Blend on high until smooth and creamy. Add more almond milk if necessary to reach your desired consistency.
4. If using, add chia seeds and pulse a few times to mix through.
5. Pour into glasses and serve immediately.

Nutritional information (approximate per serving):
Calories: 320kcal | Protein: 10g | Carbohydrates: 36g | Fat: 17g | Cholesterol: 5mg | Sodium: 120mg | Fiber: 9g | Potassium: 800mg

Greek Yogurt with Mixed Berries

Yield: 4 servings | Prep time: 5 minutes | Cook time: 0 minutes

Ingredients:
- 2 cups plain Greek yogurt
- 1 cup fresh strawberries, sliced
- 1/2 cup fresh blueberries
- 1/2 cup fresh raspberries
- 2 tablespoons honey or to taste
- Optional: mint leaves for garnish

Directions:
1. In serving bowls, divide the Greek yogurt equally.
2. Top the yogurt with an even mix of strawberries, blueberries, and raspberries.
3. Drizzle honey over the berries and yogurt to taste.

4. If desired, garnish with mint leaves for an additional pop of colour and flavour. Serve immediately.

Nutritional Information (approximate per serving):
Calories: 150 kcal | Protein: 15g | Carbohydrates: 20g | Fat: 2g | Cholesterol: 10mg | Sodium: 50mg | Fiber: 2g | Potassium: 200mg

Avocado Chocolate Smoothie with Almonds

Yield: 2 servings | Prep time: 5 minutes | Cook time: 0 minutes

Ingredients:
- 1 ripe avocado
- 2 tablespoons cocoa powder
- 2 tablespoons almond butter
- 1 tablespoon maple syrup (optional, for sweetness)
- 1 cup almond milk
- 1/4 cup almonds, chopped (for garnish)

Directions:
1. Cut the avocado in half and remove the pit. Scoop the flesh into a blender.
2. Add cocoa powder, almond butter, maple syrup (if using), and almond milk to the blender.
3. Blend until smooth and creamy.
4. Pour the smoothie into glasses and garnish with chopped almonds.
5. Serve immediately and enjoy!

Nutritional information (approximate per serving):
Calories: 314kcal | Protein: 8g | Carbohydrates: 20g | Fat: 26g | Cholesterol: 0mg | Sodium: 182mg | Fiber: 10g | Potassium: 703mg

Peanut Butter Cup Protein Shake

Yield: 2 servings | Prep time: 5 minutes | Cook time: 0 minutes

Ingredients:
- 2 cups unsweetened almond milk
- 2 scoops chocolate protein powder
- 2 tablespoons peanut butter
- 1 tablespoon cocoa powder
- 1 ripe banana
- 1 cup ice cubes

Directions:
1. In a blender, combine almond milk, chocolate protein powder, peanut butter, cocoa powder, banana, and ice cubes.
2. Blend until smooth and creamy.
3. Pour into glasses and serve immediately.

Nutritional information (approximate per serving):
Calories: 299kcal | Protein: 29g | Carbohydrates: 26g | Fat: 11g | Cholesterol: 0mg | Sodium: 306mg | Fiber: 5g | Potassium: 561mg

Berry Spinach Surprise: Mixed Berries, Spinach, and Chia Seeds

Yield: 2 servings | Prep time: 5 minutes | Cook time: 0 minutes

Ingredients:
- 1 cup mixed berries (such as strawberries, blueberries, raspberries)
- 1 cup fresh spinach leaves
- 2 tablespoons chia seeds
- 1 cup water or coconut water

Directions:
1. In a blender, combine mixed berries, fresh spinach leaves, chia seeds, and water or coconut water.
2. Blend until smooth and creamy.
3. Pour into glasses and serve immediately.

Nutritional information (approximate per serving):
Calories: 85kcal | Protein: 3g | Carbohydrates: 15g | Fat: 3g | Cholesterol: 0mg | Sodium: 10mg | Fiber: 8g | Potassium: 212mg

Berry Keto Smoothie with Raspberry and Coconut Milk

Yield: 2 servings | Prep time: 5 minutes | Cook time: 0 minutes

Ingredients:
- 1 cup frozen raspberries
- 1 cup unsweetened coconut milk
- 2 tablespoons chia seeds
- 1 tablespoon almond butter
- 1 teaspoon vanilla extract
- 1/2 cup ice cubes (optional, for extra thickness)

Directions:
1. In a blender, combine frozen raspberries, coconut milk, chia seeds, almond butter, vanilla extract, and ice cubes (if using).
2. Blend until smooth and creamy.
3. Pour into glasses and serve immediately.

Nutritional information (approximate per serving):
Calories: 170kcal | Protein: 4g | Carbohydrates: 10g | Fat: 14g | Cholesterol: 0mg | Sodium: 10mg | Fiber: 8g | Potassium: 195mg

Classic Hummus with Whole-Wheat Crackers

Yield: 4 servings | Prep time: 15 minutes | Cook time: 0 minutes

Ingredients:
- 1 can (15 ounces) chickpeas, drained and rinsed
- 1/4 cup tahini (sesame seed paste)
- 1/4 cup lemon juice
- 1 garlic clove, minced
- 2 tablespoons olive oil
- 1/2 teaspoon ground cumin
- Salt to taste
- 2 tablespoons water, or as needed
- Whole-wheat crackers for serving
- Optional garnishes: paprika, fresh parsley, additional olive oil

Directions:
1. In a food processor, combine chickpeas, tahini, lemon juice, minced garlic, olive oil, cumin, and a pinch of salt. Process until smooth.
2. While the processor is running, add water one tablespoon at a time until you reach your desired consistency.
3. Taste and adjust the seasoning if necessary.
4. Transfer the hummus to a serving bowl and, if desired, sprinkle with paprika, parsley, and a drizzle of olive oil.
5. Serve with whole-wheat crackers on the side for dipping.

Nutritional Information (approximate per serving, hummus only):
Calories: 220 kcal | Protein: 8g | Carbohydrates: 20g | Fat: 14g | Cholesterol: 0mg | Sodium: 300mg | Fibber: 5g | Potassium: 240mg

Green Tea Smoothie with Mint and Lemon

Yield: 2 servings | Prep time: 5 minutes | Cook time: 0 minutes

Ingredients:
- 1 cup brewed green tea, cooled
- 1 cup fresh spinach leaves
- 1/4 cup fresh mint leaves
- Juice of 1 lemon
- 1 tablespoon honey or maple syrup (optional, for sweetness)
- 1/2 cup ice cubes

Directions:
1. In a blender, combine brewed green tea, fresh spinach leaves, mint leaves, lemon juice, honey or maple syrup (if using), and ice cubes.
2. Blend until smooth and creamy.
3. Pour into glasses and serve immediately.

Nutritional information (approximate per serving):
Calories: 31kcal | Protein: 1g | Carbohydrates: 8g | Fat: 0g | Cholesterol: 0mg | Sodium: 22mg | Fiber: 2g | Potassium: 134mg

Multigrain Berry Bar

Yield: 6 servings | Prep time: 15 minutes | Cook time: 25 minutes

Ingredients:
- 1 cup rolled oats
- 1/2 cup whole wheat flour
- 1/2 cup mixed nuts, chopped (almonds, walnuts, pecans)
- 1/4 cup honey
- 1/4 cup unsalted butter, melted
- 1 cup mixed berries (strawberries, blueberries, raspberries), fresh or frozen
- 1/4 cup brown sugar
- 1/2 teaspoon cinnamon
- A pinch of salt

Directions:
1. Preheat the oven to 350°F (177°C). Line an 8-inch square baking pan with parchment paper, leaving some overhang for easy removal.
2. In a large bowl, mix the oats, whole wheat flour, nuts, cinnamon, and salt.
3. Stir in the melted butter and honey until the mixture is well combined.
4. Press half of the oat mixture firmly into the bottom of the prepared baking pan. Spread the berries over the top and sprinkle with brown sugar.
5. Crumble the remaining oat mixture over the berries and press down lightly.
6. Bake for 25 minutes or until the top is golden brown. Let the bars cool in the pan on a wire rack before lifting out and cutting into bars.

Nutritional Information (approximate per serving):
Calories: 280 kcal | Protein: 5g | Carbohydrates: 38g | Fat: 12g | Cholesterol: 20mg | Sodium: 30mg | Fibber: 4g | Potassium: 200mg

Classic Guacamole

Yield: 4 servings | Prep time: 10 minutes | Cook time: 0 minutes

Ingredients:
- 3 ripe avocados
- 1 lime, juiced
- 1/4 cup red onion, finely chopped
- 2 tablespoons fresh cilantro, chopped
- 1 jalapeño pepper, seeded and minced (optional)
- Salt and pepper to taste

Directions:
1. Halve the avocados, remove the pits, and scoop the flesh into a mixing bowl.
2. Add the lime juice immediately to prevent browning. Use a fork to mash the avocado to your preferred consistency.
3. Stir in the red onion, cilantro, and jalapeño (if using). Season with salt and pepper.
4. Mix well and adjust seasonings as necessary. Serve with your favorite chips or fresh veggies.

Nutritional Information (approximate per serving):
Calories: 230 kcal | Protein: 3g | Carbohydrates: 15g | Fat: 20g | Cholesterol: 0mg | Sodium: 10mg | Fibber: 10g | Potassium: 708mg

Peanut Butter and Banana Roll-Ups

Yield: 4 servings | Prep time: 10 minutes | Cook time: 0 minutes

Ingredients:
- 4 whole wheat tortillas
- 1/2 cup peanut butter
- 2 large bananas
- Optional: honey or chocolate chips for added sweetness

Directions:
1. Lay out the tortillas on a flat surface and spread each with a layer of peanut butter, leaving a small border around the edges.
2. Place a whole banana on one edge of each tortilla and roll it up tightly.
3. If desired, drizzle honey or sprinkle chocolate chips before rolling.
4. Slice each roll-up into 1-inch pieces or serve whole.

Nutritional Information (approximate per serving):
Calories: 330 kcal | Protein: 10g | Carbohydrates: 40g | Fat: 16g | Cholesterol: 0mg | Sodium: 250mg | Fiber: 6g | Potassium: 422mg

Avocado Toast with Tomato Salsa

Yield: 4 servings | Prep time: 10 minutes | Cook time: 5 minutes

Ingredients:
- 4 slices whole grain bread
- 2 ripe avocados
- 2 tomatoes, diced
- 1/4 cup diced onion
- 2 tablespoons chopped cilantro
- 1 lime, juiced
- Salt and pepper to taste

Directions:
1. Toast the slices of whole grain bread until golden brown.
2. While the bread is toasting, mash the ripe avocados in a bowl until smooth.
3. In another bowl, mix the diced tomatoes, diced onion, chopped cilantro, lime juice, salt, and pepper to make the tomato salsa.
4. Once the bread is toasted, spread the mashed avocado evenly over each slice.
5. Top the avocado toast with the prepared tomato salsa mixture.

Nutritional information (approximate per serving):
Calories: 235kcal | Protein: 5g | Carbohydrates: 22g | Fat: 16g | Cholesterol: 0mg | Sodium: 215mg

Cucumber Hummus Bite

Yield: 4 servings | Prep time: 15 minutes | Cook time: 0 minutes

Ingredients:
- 1 large cucumber
- 1/2 cup hummus
- 8 cherry tomatoes
- 8 black olives
- Fresh parsley for garnish

Directions:
1. Wash the cucumber and cut it into thick rounds, about 1/2 inch thick.
2. Use a small spoon to scoop out a small portion of the center of each cucumber round, creating a small well.
3. Fill each cucumber well with a dollop of hummus.
4. Slice the cherry tomatoes in half and place one half on top of each hummus-filled cucumber.
5. Top each cucumber bite with a slice of black olive and garnish with fresh parsley.

Nutritional information (approximate):
Calories: 58kcal | Protein: 2g | Carbohydrates: 5g | Fat: 3g | Cholesterol: 0mg | Sodium: 156mg

Fruit Kabobs with Yogurt Dip

Yield: 4 servings | Prep time: 20 minutes | Cook time: 0 minutes

Ingredients:
- 2 cups mixed fruits (such as strawberries, pineapple chunks, grapes, and melon balls)
- 4 skewers
- 1 cup Greek yogurt
- 2 tablespoons honey or maple syrup

Directions:
1. Wash and prepare the fruits as needed. Thread the mixed fruits onto skewers, alternating different fruits as desired.

2. In a small bowl, mix the Greek yogurt and honey or maple syrup until well combined to make the yogurt dip.
3. Arrange the fruit kabobs on a serving platter.
4. Serve the fruit kabobs with the prepared yogurt dip on the side for dipping.

Nutritional information (approximate per serving):
Calories: 128kcal | Protein: 6g | Carbohydrates: 26g | Fat: 0g | Cholesterol: 3mg | Sodium: 24mg

Spinach and Feta Stuffed Mushrooms

Yield: 4 servings | Prep time: 15 minutes | Cook time: 20 minutes

Ingredients:
- 12 large mushrooms
- 2 cups baby spinach, chopped
- 1/2 cup crumbled feta cheese
- 2 cloves garlic, minced
- 2 tablespoons olive oil
- Salt and pepper to taste

Directions:
1. Preheat the oven to 375°F (190°C). Clean the mushrooms and remove the stems.
2. In a skillet, heat olive oil over medium heat. Add minced garlic and chopped baby spinach, and sauté until the spinach wilts, about 2-3mins.
3. Remove the skillet from heat and stir in the crumbled feta cheese until combined.
4. Stuff each mushroom cap with the spinach and feta mixture, pressing down gently to fill.
5. Place the stuffed mushrooms on a baking sheet lined with parchment paper and bake in the preheated oven for 15-20 minutes, or until the mushrooms are tender and the filling is lightly golden.

Nutritional information (approximate per serving):
Calories: 98kcal | Protein: 5g | Carbohydrates: 5g | Fat: 7g | Cholesterol: 17mg | Sodium: 167mg

Vegetable Spring Rolls

Yield: 4 servings | Prep time: 25 minutes | Cook time: 0 minutes

Ingredients:
- 8 rice paper wrappers
- 2 cups shredded lettuce
- 1 cucumber, julienned
- 1 carrot, julienned
- 1 avocado, sliced
- 1 bell pepper, thinly sliced
- 1/4 cup fresh mint leaves
- 1/4 cup fresh cilantro leaves
- 1/4 cup low-sodium soy sauce
- 2 tablespoons lime juice

Directions:
1. Prepare all the vegetables by washing, peeling, and cutting them into thin strips.
2. Fill a shallow dish with warm water. Dip one rice paper wrapper into the water for a few seconds until it softens.
3. Lay the softened rice paper wrapper flat on a clean surface. Arrange a small amount of shredded lettuce, cucumber, carrot, avocado, bell pepper, mint leaves, and cilantro leaves in the center of the wrapper.
4. Fold the sides of the wrapper over the filling, then roll it tightly into a cylinder shape, similar to a burrito.
5. Repeat with the remaining rice paper wrappers and filling ingredients.
6. In a small bowl, mix low-sodium soy sauce and lime juice to make a dipping sauce.
7. Serve the vegetable spring rolls with the dipping sauce on the side.

Nutritional information (approximate per serving):
Calories: 172kcal | Protein: 5g | Carbohydrates: 31g | Fat: 4g | Cholesterol: 0mg | Sodium: 394mg | Fiber: 4g

Almond Berry Banana Boost

Yield: 2 servings | Prep time: 5 minutes | Cook time: 0 minutes

Ingredients:
- 1 cup unsweetened almond milk
- 1/2 cup strawberries
- 1/2 cup raspberries
- 1 ripe banana
- 1/2 cup ice
- 1 teaspoon chia seeds

Directions:
1. Combine the almond milk, strawberries, raspberries, banana, and ice in a blender.
2. Blend on high speed until all the ingredients are well combined and the mixture is smooth.
3. Add the chia seeds and pulse a few times to mix.
4. Pour into glasses and serve immediately for a refreshing and energizing smoothie.

Nutritional Information (approximate per serving):
Calories: 150 kcal | Protein: 3g | Carbohydrates: 28g | Fat: 3.5g | Cholesterol: 0mg | Sodium: 80mg | Fiber: 7g | Potassium: 422mg

Cinnamon Apple Almond Smoothie

Yield: 2 servings | Prep time: 5 minutes | Cook time: 0 minutes

Ingredients:
- 1 cup unsweetened almond milk
- 1 large apple, cored and sliced
- 1/2 teaspoon ground cinnamon
- 1 banana
- 1/4 cup raw almonds
- 1/2 cup ice
- Optional: 1 tablespoon honey or maple syrup for sweetness

Directions:
1. Place the almond milk, apple slices, banana, and almonds into a blender.
2. Add the ground cinnamon and ice.
3. Blend on high until smooth. Add honey or maple syrup if a sweeter taste is desired.
4. Pour into glasses and sprinkle a pinch of cinnamon on top for garnish if desired.

Nutritional Information (approximate per serving):
Calories: 250 kcal | Protein: 5g | Carbohydrates: 38g | Fat: 10g | Cholesterol: 0mg | Sodium: 80mg | Fiber: 7g | Potassium: 422mg

Blueberry Almond Antioxidant Smoothie

Yield: 2 servings | Prep time: 5 minutes | Cook time: 0 minutes

Ingredients:
- 1 cup unsweetened almond milk
- 3/4 cup blueberries (fresh or frozen)
- 1/2 banana, sliced
- 2 tablespoons raw almonds or almond butter
- 1/2 cup ice
- Optional: 1 tablespoon honey or maple syrup for sweetness

Directions:
1. Add the almond milk, blueberries, banana, and almonds to a blender.
2. Add ice and blend on high until smooth. If you prefer a sweeter taste, add honey or maple syrup to your liking.
3. Pour the smoothie into two glasses.
4. Serve immediately and enjoy the rich, antioxidant-packed drink.

Nutritional Information (approximate per serving):
Calories: 180 kcal | Protein: 4g | Carbohydrates: 25g | Fat: 8g | Cholesterol: 0mg | Sodium: 80mg | Fiber: 4g | Potassium: 200mg

Green Almond Energizer Smoothie

Yield: 2 servings | Prep time: 5 minutes | Cook time: 0 minutes

Ingredients:
- 1 cup unsweetened almond milk
- 1 cup baby spinach leaves
- 1 ripe banana
- 1/4 cup raw almonds or 2 tablespoons almond butter
- 1/2 green apple, cored and chopped
- 1/2 cup ice

Directions:
1. Place the almond milk, spinach, banana, almonds (or almond butter), and green apple in a blender.
2. Add the ice and blend on high until smooth and creamy.
3. Pour into glasses and serve immediately for a nutrient-rich energy boost.

Nutritional Information (approximate per serving):
Calories: 220 kcal | Protein: 5g | Carbohydrates: 26g | Fat: 11g | Cholesterol: 0mg | Sodium: 95mg | Fiber: 5g | Potassium: 400mg

Tropical Almond Delight Smoothie

Yield: 2 servings | Prep time: 5 minutes | Cook time: 0 minutes

Ingredients:
- 1 cup unsweetened almond milk
- 1/2 cup pineapple chunks
- 1/2 ripe banana
- 1/4 cup mango chunks
- 1/2 cup ice cubes
- Optional: 1 tablespoon shredded coconut for garnish

Directions:
1. Combine the almond milk, pineapple, banana, and mango in a blender.
2. Add ice cubes and blend on high until smooth and creamy.
3. Pour into two glasses and garnish with shredded coconut if desired.
4. Serve immediately and enjoy the tropical flavors.

Nutritional Information (approximate per serving):
Calories: 150 kcal | Protein: 2g | Carbohydrates: 28g | Fat: 4g | Cholesterol: 0mg | Sodium: 95mg | Fiber: 3g | Potassium: 320mg

Mango-Banana Green Smoothie

Yield: 2 servings | Prep time: 5 minutes | Cook time: 0 minutes

Ingredients:
- 1 ripe mango, peeled and chopped
- 1 ripe banana
- 1 large leaf of Swiss chard or spinach
- 1/2 cup Greek yogurt
- 1/2 cup unsweetened coconut milk
- 1 tablespoon honey or maple syrup
- Several ices cube

Directions:
1. Place the chopped mango, banana, Swiss chard or spinach leaf, Greek yogurt, coconut milk, honey or maple syrup, and ice cubes in a blender.
2. Blend until smooth and creamy.
3. Taste the smoothie and adjust sweetness, if necessary, by adding more honey or maple syrup.
4. Pour into glasses and serve immediately.

Nutritional information (approximate):
Calories: 190kcal | Protein: 6g | Carbohydrates: 34g | Fat: 4g | Cholesterol: 3mg | Sodium: 50mg

Pineapple Coconut Smoothie

Yield: 2 servings | Prep time: 5 minutes | Cook time: 0 minutes

Ingredients:
- 2 cups frozen pineapple chunks
- 1 cup coconut milk
- 1/2 cup plain Greek yogurt

- 2 tablespoons honey
- 1/4 cup shredded coconut (optional, for garnish)
- Ice cubes (optional, for a colder smoothie)

Directions:
1. In a blender, combine frozen pineapple chunks, coconut milk, Greek yogurt, and honey.
2. Blend until smooth and creamy.
3. If desired, add ice cubes and blend again until incorporated.
4. Pour into glasses, garnish with shredded coconut if desired, and serve immediately.

Nutritional Information (approximate per serving):
Calories: 254kcal | Protein: 5g | Carbohydrates: 35g | Fat: 11g | Cholesterol: 1mg | Sodium: 30mg | Fiber: 2g | Potassium: 386mg

Green Matcha Smoothie

Yield: 2 servings | Prep time: 5 minutes | Cook time: 0 minutes

Ingredients:
- 2 teaspoons matcha powder
- 1 ripe banana, frozen
- 1 cup spinach leaves
- 1 cup almond milk (or any milk of your choice)
- 1 tablespoon honey or maple syrup
- Ice cubes (optional, for a colder smoothie)

Directions:
1. In a blender, combine matcha powder, frozen banana, spinach leaves, almond milk, and honey or maple syrup.
2. Blend until smooth and creamy.
3. If desired, add ice cubes and blend again until incorporated.
4. Pour into glasses and serve immediately.

Nutritional Information (approximate per serving):
Calories: 122kcal | Protein: 3g | Carbohydrates: 27g | Fat: 2g | Cholesterol: 0mg | Sodium: 187mg | Fiber: 3g | Potassium: 375mg

Berry Beet Smoothie

Yield: 2 servings | Prep time: 5 minutes | Cook time: 0 minutes

Ingredients:
- 1 cup mixed berries (such as strawberries, blueberries, raspberries)
- 1 small beet, peeled and chopped
- 1 ripe banana
- 1 cup spinach leaves
- 1 cup almond milk (or any milk of your choice)
- 1 tablespoon honey or maple syrup
- Ice cubes (optional, for a colder smoothie)

Directions:
1. In a blender, combine mixed berries, chopped beet, banana, spinach leaves, almond milk, and honey or maple syrup.
2. Blend until smooth and creamy.
3. If desired, add ice cubes and blend again until incorporated.
4. Pour into glasses and serve immediately.

Nutritional Information (approximate per serving):
Calories: 147kcal | Protein: 3g | Carbohydrates: 32g | Fat: 2g | Cholesterol: 0mg | Sodium: 155mg | Fiber: 7g | Potassium: 579mg

Carrot Ginger Turmeric Smoothie

Yield: 2 servings | Prep time: 5 minutes | Cook time: 0 minutes

Ingredients:
- 2 large carrots, peeled and chopped
- 1-inch piece of fresh ginger, peeled and chopped
- 1 teaspoon ground turmeric
- 1 ripe banana
- 1 cup almond milk (or any milk of your choice)
- 1 tablespoon honey or maple syrup
- Ice cubes (optional, for a colder smoothie)

Directions:
1. In a blender, combine chopped carrots, ginger, turmeric, banana, almond milk, and honey or maple syrup.
2. Blend until smooth and creamy.
3. If desired, add ice cubes and blend again until incorporated.
4. Pour into glasses and serve immediately.

Nutritional Information: Calories: 154 | Protein: 2g | Carbohydrates: 36g | Fat: 2g | Cholesterol: 0mg | Sodium: 176mg | Fiber: 6g | Potassium: 503mg

Salads

Kale and Quinoa Salad with Lemon-Tahini Dressing

Yield: 4 servings | Prep time: 15 minutes | Cook time: 0 minutes

Ingredients:
- 2 cups chopped kale; stems removed
- 1/2 cup cooked quinoa
- 1/4 cup dried cranberries
- 1/4 cup sliced almonds
- 1/4 cup pumpkin seeds

   Dressing:
- 2 tablespoons tahini
- 1 tablespoon lemon juice
- 1 garlic clove, minced
- Salt and pepper to taste
- Water to thin (as needed)

Nutritional information (approximate per serving):
Calories: 350 kcal | Protein: 10g | Carbohydrates: 40g | Fat: 18g | Cholesterol: 0mg | Sodium: 120mg | Fiber: 6g | Potassium: 450mg

Spinach and Berry Salad with Poppy Seed Dressing

Yield: 4 servings | Prep time: 15 minutes | Cook time: 0 minutes

Ingredients:
- 2 cups fresh spinach leaves
- 1/2 cup sliced strawberries
- 1/2 cup blueberries
- 1/4 cup feta cheese crumbles
- 1/4 cup walnuts, toasted

Dressing:
- 2 tablespoons Greek yogurt
- 1 tablespoon olive oil
- 1 tablespoon honey
- 1 teaspoon poppy seeds

Nutritional information (approximate per serving):
Calories: 280 kcal | Protein: 6g | Carbohydrates: 22g | Fat: 20g | Cholesterol: 15mg | Sodium: 250mg | Fiber: 4g | Potassium: 380mg

Avocado and Black Bean Salad with Cilantro-Lime Dressing

Yield: 4 servings | Prep time: 15 minutes | Cook time: 0 minutes

Ingredients:
- 1 ripe avocado, diced
- 1/2 cup black beans, rinsed and drained
- 1/2 cup corn kernels
- 1/4 cup cherry tomatoes, halved
- 1/4 cup red onion, finely chopped

Dressing:
- 2 tablespoons lime juice
- 1/4 cup fresh cilantro, chopped
- 1 tablespoon extra-virgin olive oil
- Salt and pepper to taste

Nutritional information (approximate per serving):
Calories: 300 kcal | Protein: 8g | Carbohydrates: 30g | Fat: 18g | Cholesterol: 0mg | Sodium: 200mg | Fiber: 10g | Potassium: 700mg

Mixed Greens with Apple and Walnut Vinaigrette

Yield: 4 servings | Prep time: 15 minutes | Cook time: 0 minutes

Ingredients:
- 2 cups mixed greens (lettuce, arugula, spinach)
- 1 apple, thinly sliced
- 1/4 cup goat cheese, crumbled
- 1/4 cup walnuts, chopped

Dressing:
- 2 tablespoons walnut oil
- 1 tablespoon apple cider vinegar
- 1 teaspoon Dijon mustard
- Salt and pepper to taste

Nutritional information (approximate per serving):
Calories: 250 kcal | Protein: 5g | Carbohydrates: 15g | Fat: 20g | Cholesterol: 10mg | Sodium: 200mg | Fiber: 3g | Potassium: 300mg

Mediterranean Chickpea Salad with Herb Dressing

Yield: 4 servings | Prep time: 15 minutes | Cook time: 0 minutes

Ingredients:
- 2 cups mixed greens
- 1/2 cup chickpeas, rinsed and drained
- 1/4 cup Kalamata olives, pitted and sliced
- 1/4 cup diced cucumber
- 1/4 cup diced bell pepper

Dressing:
- 2 tablespoons olive oil
- 1 tablespoon red wine vinegar
- 1/2 teaspoon dried oregano
- 1/2 teaspoon dried basil
- Salt and pepper to taste

Nutritional information (approximate per serving):
Calories: 280 kcal | Protein: 7g | Carbohydrates: 25g | Fat: 18g | Cholesterol: 0mg | Sodium: 400mg, Fiber: 6g | Potassium: 350mg

Crunchy Cabbage Slaw with Sesame Ginger Dressing

Yield: 4 servings | Prep time: 15 minutes | Cook time: 0 minutes

Ingredients:
- 2 cups shredded red cabbage
- 1 cup shredded carrots
- 1/4 cup sliced green onions
- 1 cup sliced almonds
- 1 tablespoon sesame seeds

Dressing:
- 2 tablespoons sesame oil
- 1 tablespoon rice vinegar
- 1 teaspoon grated ginger
- 1 teaspoon soy sauce
- 1 teaspoon honey

Nutritional information (approximate per serving):
Calories: 190 kcal | Protein: 3g | Carbohydrates: 14g | Fat: 14g | Cholesterol: 0mg | Sodium: 150mg | Fiber: 3g | Potassium: 300mg

Roasted Beet and Goat Cheese Salad with Balsamic Reduction

Yield: 4 servings | Prep time: 15 minutes | Cook time: 0 minutes

Ingredients:
- 2 cups arugula
- 1/2 cup roasted beets, sliced
- 1/4 cup goat cheese, crumbled
- 1/4 cup pecans, toasted

Dressing:
- 2 tablespoons balsamic reduction
- 1 tablespoon olive oil
- Salt and pepper to taste

Nutritional information (approximate per serving):
Calories: 220 kcal | Protein: 6g | Carbohydrates: 10g | Fat: 18g | Cholesterol: 13mg | Sodium: 180mg | Fiber: 2g | Potassium: 350mg

Summer Berry Spinach Salad with Honey Lime Dressing

Yield: 4 servings | Prep time: 15 minutes | Cook time: 0 minutes

Ingredients:
- 2 cups baby spinach
- 1/2 cup mixed berries (strawberries, blueberries, raspberries)
- 1/4 cup feta cheese, crumbled
- 1/4 cup slivered almonds

Dressing:
- 2 tablespoons lime juice
- 1 tablespoon honey
- 1 tablespoon olive oil
- Mint leaves for garnish

Nutritional information (approximate per serving):
Calories: 200 kcal | Protein: 5g | Carbohydrates: 18g | Fat: 13g | Cholesterol: 15mg | Sodium: 200mg | Fiber: 4g | Potassium: 400mg

Greek Salad with Herb Marinated Olives

Yield: 4 servings | Prep time: 15 minutes | Cook time: 0 minutes

Ingredients:
- 2 cups romaine lettuce, chopped
- 1/4 cup cherry tomatoes, halved
- 1/4 cup cucumber, sliced
- 1/4 cup red onion, thinly sliced
- 1/4 cup crumbled feta cheese
- 2 tablespoons marinated olives

Dressing:
- 2 tablespoons olive oil
- 1 tablespoon lemon juice
- 1/2 teaspoon dried oregano
- Salt and pepper to taste

Nutritional information (approximate per serving):
Calories: 180 kcal | Protein: 4g | Carbohydrates: 8g | Fat: 15g | Cholesterol: 25mg | Sodium: 350mg | Fiber: 2g | Potassium: 200mg

Chickpea and Quinoa Salad

Yield: 4 servings | Prep time: 15 minutes | Cook time: 15 minutes

Ingredients:
- 1 cup quinoa
- 1 can (15 ounces) chickpeas, drained and rinsed
- 1 bell pepper, diced
- 1 cucumber, diced
- 1/4 cup red onion, finely chopped
- 1/4 cup fresh parsley, chopped
- 1/4 cup olive oil
- 2 tablespoons lemon juice
- 1 teaspoon ground cumin
- Salt and pepper, to taste

Directions:
1. Rinse the quinoa under cold water and cook according to package instructions. Once cooked, fluff with a fork and let it cool.
2. In a large mixing bowl, combine the cooked quinoa, chickpeas, diced bell pepper, diced cucumber, chopped red onion, and chopped parsley.
3. In a small bowl, whisk together the olive oil, lemon juice, ground cumin, salt, and pepper to make the dressing.
4. Pour the dressing over the salad ingredients and toss until everything is evenly coated.
5. Serve immediately or refrigerate until ready to serve.

Nutritional information (approximate):
Calories: 345kcal | Protein: 11g | Carbohydrates: 48g | Fat: 13g | Cholesterol: 0mg | Sodium: 390mg | Fiber: 9g | Potassium: 532mg

Southwest Quinoa and Black Bean Salad with Avocado Lime Dressing

Yield: 4 servings | Prep time: 15 minutes | Cook time: 0 minutes

Ingredients:
- 1 cup cooked quinoa
- 1/2 cup black beans, rinsed and drained
- 1/2 cup corn, roasted or grilled
- 1/4 cup red bell pepper, diced
- 1 avocado, diced

Dressing:
- 2 tablespoons lime juice
- 1/4 cup avocado
- 1/4 teaspoon cumin
- Salt and pepper to taste
- Water to thin, as needed

Nutritional information (approximate per serving):
Calories: 320 kcal | Protein: 9g | Carbohydrates: 45g | Fat: 12g | Cholesterol: 0mg | Sodium: 200mg | Fiber: 9g | Potassium: 600mg

Mango Avocado Salad with Honey Lime Dressing

Yield: 4 servings | Prep time: 15 minutes | Cook time: 0 minutes

Ingredients:
- 2 ripe mangos, diced
- 2 ripe avocados, diced
- 1/4 cup red onion, thinly sliced
- 1/4 cup fresh cilantro, chopped
- 1/4 cup toasted sliced almonds
- Mixed greens (such as spinach, arugula, and romaine)

For the Honey Lime Dressing:
- 3 tablespoons olive oil
- 2 tablespoons lime juice
- 1 tablespoon honey
- 1 teaspoon Dijon mustard
- Salt and pepper to taste

Directions:
1. In a large salad bowl, combine the diced mangos, avocados, red onion, chopped cilantro, and toasted sliced almonds.
2. In a small bowl, whisk together the olive oil, lime juice, honey, Dijon mustard, salt, and pepper to make the dressing.
3. Pour the dressing over the mango avocado mixture and gently toss to coat evenly.
4. Arrange a bed of mixed greens on serving plates or in a large salad bowl.
5. Spoon the mango avocado mixture over the greens.
6. Serve immediately and enjoy this refreshing and flavorful salad!

Nutritional information (approximate):
Calories: 320kcal | Protein: 5g | Carbohydrates: 26g | Fat: 24g | Cholesterol: 0mg | Sodium: 40mg | Fiber: 8g | Potassium: 800mg

Tomato Basil Mozzarella Salad

Yield: 4 servings | Prep time: 15 minutes | Cook time: 0 minutes

Ingredients:
- 2 large tomatoes, sliced
- 1 cup fresh mozzarella balls, halved
- 1/4 cup fresh basil leaves, torn
- 2 tablespoons extra virgin olive oil
- 1 tablespoon balsamic vinegar
- Salt and pepper to taste

Directions:
1. In a large bowl, combine the sliced tomatoes, mozzarella balls, and torn basil leaves.
2. Drizzle olive oil and balsamic vinegar over the salad.
3. Season with salt and pepper to taste. Toss gently to combine.

Nutritional Information (approximate per serving):
Calories: 180-300kcal | Protein: 8-15g | Carbohydrates: 4-8g | Fat: 14-23g | Cholesterol: 30-50mg | Sodium: 200-400mg | Fiber: 1-2g | Potassium: 250-500mg

Cucumber Tomato Salad with Cilantro and Lime

Yield: 4 servings | Prep time: 15 minutes | Cook time: 0 minutes

Ingredients:
- 2 large cucumbers, diced
- 2 large tomatoes, diced
- 1/4 cup fresh cilantro, chopped
- Juice of 1 lime
- Salt and pepper to taste

Directions:
1. In a large bowl, combine the diced cucumbers, tomatoes, and chopped cilantro.
2. Squeeze the lime juice over the salad.
3. Season with salt and pepper to taste. Toss gently to combine.

Nutritional Information (approximate per serving):
Calories: 30-50kcal | Protein: 1-2g | Carbohydrates: 6-10g | Fat: 0-1g | Cholesterol: 0mg | Sodium: 5-10mg | Fiber: 1-2g | Potassium: 150-250mg

Arugula and Pear Salad

Yield: 4 servings | Prep time: 10 minutes | Cook time: 0 minutes

Ingredients:
- 4 cups arugula
- 2 ripe pears, thinly sliced
- 1/4 cup walnuts, chopped
- 1/4 cup crumbled goat cheese
- 2 tablespoons extra virgin olive oil
- 1 tablespoon balsamic vinegar
- Salt and pepper to taste

Directions:
1. In a large bowl, toss together the arugula, sliced pears, chopped walnuts, and crumbled goat cheese.
2. Drizzle the olive oil and balsamic vinegar over the salad.
3. Season with salt and pepper to taste. Toss gently to combine.

Nutritional Information (approximate per serving):
Calories: 150-250kcal | Protein: 3-5g | Carbohydrates: 12-20g | Fat: 10-15g | Cholesterol: 5-10mg | Sodium: 50-100mg | Fiber: 3-5g | Potassium: 250-400mg

Broccoli Cranberry Salad

Yield: 4 servings | Prep time: 15 minutes | Cook time: 0 minutes

Ingredients:
- 4 cups broccoli florets
- 1/2 cup dried cranberries

- 1/4 cup chopped red onion
- 1/4 cup chopped pecans
- 1/4 cup mayonnaise
- 2 tablespoons apple cider vinegar
- 1 tablespoon honey
- Salt and pepper to taste

Directions
1. In a large bowl, combine the broccoli florets, dried cranberries, chopped red onion, and chopped pecans.
2. In a small bowl, whisk together the mayonnaise, apple cider vinegar, honey, salt, and pepper.
3. Pour the dressing over the broccoli mixture and toss until evenly coated. Serve chilled.

Nutritional Information (approximate per serving):
Calories: 150-250kcal | Protein: 2-4g | Carbohydrates: 15-25g | Fat: 8-12g | Cholesterol: 0-5mg | Sodium: 100-200mg | Fiber: 3-5g | Potassium: 250-400mg

Cucumber Yogurt Salad

Yield: 4 servings | Prep time: 10 minutes | Cook time: 0 minutes

Ingredients:
- 2 large cucumbers, thinly sliced
- 1 cup plain Greek yogurt
- 2 tablespoons fresh dill, chopped
- 1 tablespoon lemon juice
- 1 clove garlic, minced
- Salt and pepper to taste

Directions:
1. In a large bowl, combine the thinly sliced cucumbers, Greek yogurt, chopped dill, lemon juice, and minced garlic.
2. Season with salt and pepper to taste. Toss gently to combine.
3. Serve chilled.

Nutritional Information (approximate per serving):
Calories: 50-100kcal | Protein: 3-6g | Carbohydrates: 5-10g | Fat: 1-3g | Cholesterol: 0-5mg | Sodium: 30-60mg | Fiber: 1-2g | Potassium: 150-300mg

Warm Cauliflower Salad

Yield: 4 servings | Prep time: 10 minutes | Cook time: 20 minutes

Ingredients:
- 1 head cauliflower, cut into florets
- 2 tablespoons olive oil
- 2 cloves garlic, minced
- 1 teaspoon smoked paprika
- 1/2 teaspoon cumin
- Salt and pepper to taste
- 1/4 cup chopped fresh parsley
- 1/4 cup crumbled feta cheese

Directions:
1. Preheat the oven to 400°F (200°C).
2. In a large bowl, toss the cauliflower florets with olive oil, minced garlic, smoked paprika, cumin, salt, and pepper until evenly coated.
3. Spread the cauliflower in a single layer on a baking sheet and roast for 20 minutes, or until golden brown and tender.
4. Transfer the roasted cauliflower to a serving bowl. Sprinkle with chopped parsley and crumbled feta cheese.
5. Serve warm.

Nutritional Information (approximate per serving):
Calories: 80-150kcal | Protein: 3-6g | Carbohydrates: 5-10g | Fat: 5-10g | Cholesterol: 5-10mg | Sodium: 150-300mg | Fiber: 3-5g | Potassium: 250-400mg

Avocado Caprese Salad

Yield: 4 servings | Prep time: 10 minutes | Cook time: 0 minutes

Ingredients:
- 2 ripe avocados, sliced
- 2 large tomatoes, sliced
- 1 cup fresh mozzarella balls, halved
- 1/4 cup fresh basil leaves
- 2 tablespoons balsamic glaze
- Salt and pepper to taste

Directions:
1. Arrange the sliced avocados, tomatoes, and mozzarella balls on a serving platter.
2. Scatter fresh basil leaves over the top.
3. Drizzle balsamic glaze over the salad.
4. Season with salt and pepper to taste.

Nutritional Information (approximate per serving):
Calories: 200-350kcal | Protein: 8-15g | Carbohydrates: 10-15g | Fat: 15-25g | Cholesterol: 10-20mg | Sodium: 200-400mg | Fiber: 5-8g | Potassium: 500-800mg

Vegetarian Niçoise Salad

Yield: 4 servings | Prep time: 15 minutes | Cook time: 15 minutes

Ingredients:
- 1 head lettuce, washed and torn
- 1 cup cherry tomatoes, halved
- 1 cup green beans, trimmed and blanched
- 4 hard-boiled eggs, halved
- 1/2 cup pitted Niçoise olives
- 1/4 cup sliced red onion
- 1/4 cup capers
- 1/4 cup chopped fresh parsley
- 1/4 cup extra virgin olive oil
- 2 tablespoons red wine vinegar
- 1 teaspoon Dijon mustard
- Salt and pepper to taste

Directions:
1. Arrange the torn lettuce on a serving platter.
2. Top with halved cherry tomatoes, blanched green beans, halved hard-boiled eggs, Niçoise olives, sliced red onion, capers, and chopped fresh parsley.
3. In a small bowl, whisk together the olive oil, red wine vinegar, Dijon mustard, salt, and pepper to make the dressing.
4. Drizzle the dressing over the salad just before serving.

Nutritional Information (approximate per serving):
Calories: 200-350kcal | Protein: 8-15g | Carbohydrates: 10-15g | Fat: 15-25g | Cholesterol: 200-400mg | Sodium: 500-800mg | Fiber: 5-8g | Potassium: 500-800mg

Soups

Classic Vegetable Soup

Yield: 4 servings | Prep time: 15 minutes | Cook time: 30 minutes

Ingredients:
- 1 tablespoon olive oil
- 1 medium onion, diced
- 2 carrots, peeled and chopped
- 2 stalks celery, chopped
- 1 small zucchini, chopped
- 2 cloves garlic, minced
- 1 can (14.5 ounces) diced tomatoes; no salt added
- 4 cups low-sodium vegetable broth
- 1 cup green beans, trimmed and cut into 1-inch pieces
- 1 teaspoon dried basil
- Salt and pepper to taste

Directions:
1. Heat the olive oil in a large pot over medium heat. Add the onions, carrots, and celery, and cook until softened, about 5 minutes.
2. Add the zucchini and garlic and cook for another 2 minutes.
3. Stir in the canned tomatoes with their juice and the vegetable broth. Bring to a simmer.
4. Add the green beans and dried basil. Season with salt and pepper to taste. Simmer for 20 minutes or until the vegetables are tender.
5. Adjust seasonings if necessary and serve hot.

Nutritional Information (approximate per serving):
Calories: 120 kcal | Protein: 3g | Carbohydrates: 22g | Fat: 3g | Cholesterol: 0mg | Sodium: 300mg | Fiber: 5g | Potassium: 400mg

Butternut Squash Soup

Yield: 4 servings | Prep time: 20 minutes | Cook time: 45 minutes

Ingredients:
- 1 large butternut squash (about 3 pounds), peeled, seeded, and cut into 1-inch cubes
- 2 tablespoons olive oil
- 1 medium onion, diced
- 2 cloves garlic, minced
- 4 cups low-sodium vegetable broth
- 1/2 teaspoon dried thyme
- Salt and pepper to taste
- Optional garnish: a dollop of plain Greek yogurt and a sprinkle of fresh parsley

Directions:
1. In a large pot, heat olive oil over medium heat. Add the onion and garlic, and sauté until softened, about 5 minutes.
2. Add the cubed butternut squash, vegetable broth, and dried thyme. Season with salt and pepper.
3. Bring to a boil, then reduce heat to a simmer and cover. Cook until the squash is tender, about 30 minutes.
4. Use an immersion blender to purée the soup until smooth (or transfer to a blender in batches, being careful with the hot liquid).
5. Taste and adjust seasoning as needed. Serve hot with an optional dollop of Greek yogurt and a sprinkle of fresh parsley for garnish.

Nutritional Information (approximate per serving):
Calories: 180 kcal | Protein: 3g | Carbohydrates: 39g | Fat: 4.5g | Cholesterol: 0mg | Sodium: 300mg | Fiber: 6g | Potassium: 582mg

Tomato Basil Soup

Yield: 4 servings | Prep time: 10 minutes | Cook time: 30 minutes

Ingredients:
- 2 tablespoons olive oil
- 1 medium onion, finely chopped
- 3 cloves of garlic, minced
- 2 cans (14.5 ounces each) no-salt-added diced tomatoes
- 1 can (15 ounces) tomato sauce
- 4 cups low-sodium vegetable broth
- 1/4 cup fresh basil leaves, chopped
- Salt and freshly ground black pepper to taste
- Optional: a drizzle of balsamic vinegar

Directions:
1. In a large pot, heat the olive oil over medium heat. Add the onion and garlic and sauté until translucent, about 5 minutes.
2. Pour in the diced tomatoes with their juice and the tomato sauce. Add the vegetable broth and bring the mixture to a simmer.
3. Stir in the chopped basil, salt, and pepper. Let the soup simmer for 20 minutes, allowing the flavors to meld together.
4. Using an immersion blender, purée the soup directly in the pot until smooth. Alternatively, carefully transfer to a blender to purée in batches.
5. Serve hot, with a drizzle of balsamic vinegar if desired.

Nutritional Information (approximate per serving):
Calories: 150 kcal | Protein: 3g | Carbohydrates: 18g | Fat: 8g | Cholesterol: 0mg | Sodium: 300mg | Fiber: 4g | Potassium: 550mg

Chickpea and Spinach Soup

Yield: 4 servings | Prep time: 10 minutes | Cook time: 25 minutes

Ingredients:
- 1 tablespoon olive oil
- 1 large onion, diced
- 2 garlic cloves, minced
- 1 can (15 ounces) chickpeas, drained and rinsed
- 4 cups low-sodium vegetable broth
- 2 cups fresh spinach, roughly chopped
- 1 teaspoon smoked paprika
- 1/2 teaspoon ground cumin
- Salt and pepper to taste
- Lemon wedges for serving

Directions:
1. Heat olive oil in a large pot over medium heat. Add onion and garlic, cooking until the onion is translucent, about 3-4 minutes.
2. Stir in the smoked paprika, ground cumin, salt, and pepper, cooking for another minute until fragrant.
3. Add the chickpeas and vegetable broth. Increase heat to bring to a boil, then reduce to a simmer for 15 minutes.
4. Add the fresh spinach and cook until wilted, about 2 minutes.
5. Optional: Use an immersion blender to blend part of the soup if a thicker consistency is desired.
6. Serve hot with a squeeze of lemon juice.

Nutritional Information (approximate per serving):
Calories: 190 kcal | Protein: 7g | Carbohydrates: 30g | Fat: 5g | Cholesterol: 0mg | Sodium: 300mg | Fiber: 8g | Potassium: 470mg

Mushroom Barley Soup

Yield: 4 servings | Prep time: 15 minutes | Cook time: 60 minutes

Ingredients:
- 1 tablespoon olive oil
- 1 onion, finely chopped

- 2 cloves garlic, minced
- 1 carrot, peeled and diced
- 1 celery stalk, diced
- 8 ounces mushrooms, sliced
- 3/4 cup pearl barley, rinsed
- 6 cups low-sodium vegetable broth
- 1 teaspoon dried thyme
- Salt and pepper to taste
- Fresh parsley, chopped for garnish

Directions:
1. Heat the olive oil in a large pot over medium heat. Add the onion and garlic, and sauté until translucent, about 5 minutes.
2. Add the carrot and celery and cook for another 5 minutes until they start to soften.
3. Stir in the mushrooms and cook until they release their moisture and begin to brown, about 8 minutes.
4. Add the barley, vegetable broth, and dried thyme. Season with salt and pepper to taste.
5. Bring to a boil, then reduce heat to a simmer. Cover and cook until the barley is tender, about 45 minutes.
6. Adjust seasoning, if necessary, garnish with fresh parsley, and serve hot.

Nutritional Information (approximate per serving):
Calories: 240 kcal | Protein: 8g | Carbohydrates: 44g | Fat: 4g | Cholesterol: 0mg | Sodium: 200mg |

Creamy Potato Leek Soup

Yield: 4 servings | Prep time: 10 minutes | Cook time: 30 minutes

Ingredients:
- 3 large leeks, white and light green parts only, cleaned and thinly sliced
- 2 tablespoons unsalted butter
- 4 cups low-sodium chicken or vegetable broth
- 2 pounds potatoes (such as Yukon gold), peeled and diced
- 1 bay leaf
- 1 teaspoon dried thyme
- Salt and pepper to taste
- 1/2 cup heavy cream or half-and-half (optional for creaminess)
- Chopped chives for garnish

Directions:
1. In a large pot, melt the butter over medium heat. Add the leeks and a pinch of salt. Cook, stirring occasionally, until leeks are soft, about 5-7 minutes.
2. Add the diced potatoes, broth, bay leaf, and thyme. Season with salt and pepper. Bring to a boil, then lower the heat and simmer for about 20 minutes or until the potatoes are tender.
3. Remove the bay leaf. Use an immersion blender to puree the soup until smooth (or blend in batches using a regular blender).
4. If using, stir in the heavy cream and heat through. Adjust the seasoning if needed.
5. Serve hot, garnished with chopped chives.

Nutritional Information (approximate per serving):
Calories: 260 kcal | Protein: 6g | Carbohydrates 48g | Fat: 5g (without heavy cream) | Cholesterol: 15mg (without heavy cream) | Sodium: 300mg | Fiber: 6g | Potassium: 900mg

Creamy Broccoli and Cauliflower Soup

Yield: 4 servings | Prep time: 15 minutes | Cook time: 25 minutes

Ingredients:
- 1 tablespoon olive oil
- 1 medium onion, chopped
- 2 cloves garlic, minced
- 2 cups broccoli florets
- 2 cups cauliflower florets
- 4 cups low-sodium vegetable broth
- 1/2 cup milk or a non-dairy alternative
- Salt and pepper to taste
- Optional: shredded cheese for garnish

Directions:
1. In a large pot, heat olive oil over medium heat. Add onion and garlic, sautéing until softened, about 5 minutes.

2. Add broccoli and cauliflower florets to the pot, cooking for another 2-3 minutes.
3. Pour in the vegetable broth and bring the mixture to a simmer. Cover and cook until the vegetables are tender, about 15 minutes.
4. Remove from heat and blend the soup using an immersion blender until smooth. Alternatively, carefully transfer to a stand blender in batches.
5. Stir in the milk, and season with salt and pepper to taste. Warm the soup over low heat if needed.
6. Serve hot, garnished with shredded cheese if desired.

Nutritional Information (approximate per serving):
Calories: 120 kcal | Protein: 5g | Carbohydrates: 15g | Fat: 5g | Cholesterol: 5mg | Sodium: 200mg | Fiber: 4g | Potassium: 450mg

Carrot Ginger Soup

Yield: 4 servings | Prep time: 15 minutes | Cook time: 35 minutes

Ingredients:
- 2 tablespoons olive oil
- 1 onion, diced
- 2 tablespoons fresh ginger, grated
- 4 cups carrots, peeled and chopped
- 4 cups low-sodium vegetable broth
- Salt and pepper to taste
- Optional: coconut milk for garnish
- Optional: fresh herbs for garnish

Directions:
1. Heat the olive oil in a large pot over medium heat. Add the onions and ginger, and sauté until the onions are translucent, about 5 minutes.
2. Add the chopped carrots to the pot and cook for an additional 5 minutes, stirring occasionally.
3. Pour in the vegetable broth and bring to a boil. Reduce heat to a simmer, cover, and cook until the carrots are soft, about 25 minutes.
4. Use an immersion blender to puree the soup until smooth. Alternatively, transfer to a blender in batches and blend until smooth.
5. Season with salt and pepper to taste. If desired, swirl in a tablespoon of coconut milk for added creaminess and garnish with fresh herbs.
6. Serve hot.

Nutritional Information (approximate per serving):
Calories: 140 kcal | Protein: 2g | Carbohydrates: 19g | Fat: 7g | Cholesterol: 0mg | Sodium: 300mg | Fiber: 5g, Potassium: 470mg

Golden Lentil and Spinach Soup

Yield: 4 servings | Prep time: 15 minutes | Cook time: 30 minutes

Ingredients:
- 1 cup dry red lentils
- 1 tablespoon olive oil
- 1 onion, chopped
- 2 cloves garlic, minced
- 1 teaspoon ground turmeric
- 1 teaspoon ground cumin
- 1/2 teaspoon ground coriander
- 1/4 teaspoon cayenne pepper (optional, for heat)
- 4 cups vegetable broth
- 1 can (14 ounces) diced tomatoes
- 2 cups fresh spinach leaves
- Salt and pepper, to taste
- Fresh cilantro, for garnish (optional)

Directions:
1. Rinse the lentils under cold water until the water runs clear. Set aside.
2. In a large pot, heat the olive oil over medium heat. Add the chopped onion and garlic, and sauté until softened, about 5 minutes.
3. Stir in the turmeric, cumin, coriander, and cayenne pepper (if using), and cook for an additional minute until fragrant.
4. Add the rinsed lentils, vegetable broth, and diced tomatoes to the pot. Bring to a simmer and cook for 20-25 minutes, or until the lentils are tender.
5. Stir in the fresh spinach leaves and cook for another 2-3 minutes until wilted. Season with salt and pepper to taste.

6. Serve hot, garnished with fresh cilantro if desired.

Nutritional information (approximate per serving):
Calories: 263kcal | Protein: 15g | Carbohydrates: 41g | Fat: 4g | Cholesterol: 0mg | Sodium: 996mg | Fiber: 15g | Potassium: 811mg

Vegetable Quinoa Soup

Yield: 4 servings | Prep time: 15 minutes | Cook time: 25 minutes

Ingredients:
- 1 tablespoon olive oil
- 1 onion, chopped
- 2 carrots, diced
- 2 celery stalks, diced
- 2 cloves garlic, minced
- 1 teaspoon dried thyme
- 1 teaspoon dried oregano
- 1/2 teaspoon paprika
- 1/2 cup quinoa, rinsed
- 4 cups vegetable broth
- 1 can (14 ounces) diced tomatoes
- 2 cups chopped mixed vegetables (such as bell peppers, zucchini, and broccoli)
- Salt and pepper, to taste
- Fresh parsley, for garnish (optional)

Directions:
1. In a large pot, heat the olive oil over medium heat. Add the chopped onion, carrots, and celery, and sauté until softened, about 5 minutes.
2. Add the minced garlic, dried thyme, dried oregano, and paprika to the pot. Cook for an additional minute until fragrant.
3. Stir in the rinsed quinoa, vegetable broth, and diced tomatoes. Bring to a simmer and cook for 15 minutes.
4. Add the chopped mixed vegetables to the pot and continue to cook for another 8-10 minutes, or until the quinoa and vegetables are tender.
5. Season the soup with salt and pepper to taste. Serve hot, garnished with fresh parsley if desired.

Nutritional information (approximate per serving):
Calories: 231kcal | Protein: 7g | Carbohydrates: 37g | Fat: 7g | Cholesterol: 0mg | Sodium: 942mg | Fiber: 7g | Potassium: 585mg

Miso Soup with Tofu and Seaweed

Yield: 4 servings | Prep time: 10 minutes | Cook time: 10 minutes

Ingredients:
- 4 cups water
- 4 tablespoons miso paste
- 1 block (14 ounces) firm tofu, cubed
- 2 sheets dried seaweed (nori), torn into small pieces
- 2 green onions, thinly sliced
- 1 tablespoon soy sauce
- 1 teaspoon sesame oil
- Optional: sliced mushrooms, thinly sliced carrots, or other vegetables of choice

Directions:
1. In a pot, bring the water to a simmer over medium heat.
2. Dissolve the miso paste in a small bowl with a ladleful of the hot water, then pour the mixture back into the pot.
3. Add the tofu, seaweed, green onions, soy sauce, and sesame oil to the pot. If using additional vegetables, add them at this point.
4. Simmer the soup for about 5 minutes, or until the tofu is heated through and the seaweed is tender.
5. Taste and adjust seasoning if necessary. Serve hot.

Nutritional information (approximat per serving e):
Calories: 162kcal | Protein: 12g | Carbohydrates: 9g | Fat: 9g | Cholesterol: 0mg | Sodium: 1183mg | Fiber: 2g | Potassium: 324mg

Kale and White Bean Soup

Yield: 4 servings | Prep time: 10 minutes | Cook time: 20 minutes

Ingredients:
- 1 tablespoon olive oil
- 1 onion, diced
- 2 cloves garlic, minced
- 4 cups vegetable broth
- 2 cups chopped kale, stems removed
- 1 can (15 oz) white beans, drained and rinsed
- Salt and pepper to taste

Directions:
1. Heat olive oil in a large pot over medium heat. Add diced onion and minced garlic, sauté until softened, about 5 minutes.
2. Pour in vegetable broth and bring to a simmer.
3. Add chopped kale and white beans to the pot. Cook for about 10 minutes until kale is wilted and beans are heated through.
4. Season with salt and pepper to taste.

Nutritional Information (approximate per serving):
Calories: 180-300kcal | Protein: 8-16g | Carbohydrates: 25-45g | Fat: 5-10g | Cholesterol: 0mg | Sodium: 600-1200mg | Fiber: 6-12g | Potassium: 400-800mg

Spicy Black Bean Soup

Yield: 4 servings | Prep time: 10 minutes | Cook time: 25 minutes

Ingredients:
- 1 tablespoon olive oil
- 1 onion, diced
- 2 cloves garlic, minced
- 1 red bell pepper, diced
- 1 jalapeño pepper, seeded and minced
- 2 teaspoons ground cumin
- 1 teaspoon chili powder
- 2 cans (15 oz each) black beans, drained and rinsed
- 4 cups vegetable broth
- Salt and pepper to taste
- Optional toppings: diced avocado, chopped cilantro, sour cream, shredded cheese

Directions:
1. In a large pot, heat olive oil over medium heat. Add diced onion, minced garlic, diced red bell pepper, and minced jalapeño pepper. Sauté until vegetables are softened, about 5 minutes.
2. Stir in ground cumin and chili powder, cook for another minute until fragrant.
3. Add black beans and vegetable broth to the pot. Bring to a simmer and let cook for about 15 minutes.
4. Use an immersion blender to blend the soup until smooth, or transfer soup to a blender and blend in batches until smooth.
5. Season with salt and pepper to taste. Serve hot with optional toppings if desired.

Nutritional Information (approximate per serving):
Calories: 200-400kcal | Protein: 8-16g | Carbohydrates: 30-60g | Fat: 5-10g | Cholesterol: 0mg | Sodium: 600-1200mg | Fiber: 8-16g | Potassium: 600-1200mg

Sweet Corn and Zucchini Soup

Yield: 4 servings | Prep time: 10 minutes | Cook time: 20 minutes

Ingredients:
- 1 tablespoon olive oil
- 1 onion, diced
- 2 cloves garlic, minced
- 2 medium zucchini, diced
- 2 cups sweet corn kernels (fresh or frozen)
- 4 cups vegetable broth
- Salt and pepper to taste
- Optional garnish: chopped fresh parsley or cilantro

Directions:
1. Heat olive oil in a large pot over medium heat. Add diced onion and minced garlic, sauté until softened, about 5 minutes.

2. Add diced zucchini to the pot and cook for another 5 minutes until slightly tender.
3. Stir in sweet corn kernels and vegetable broth. Bring to a simmer and let cook for about 10 minutes.
4. Use an immersion blender to blend the soup until smooth, or transfer soup to a blender and blend in batches until smooth.
5. Season with salt and pepper to taste. Serve hot, garnished with chopped fresh parsley or cilantro if desired.

Nutritional Information (approximate per serving):
Calories: 150-250kcal | Protein: 4-8g | Carbohydrates: 20-40g | Fat: 5-10g, Cholesterol: 0mg | Sodium: 600-1200mg | Fiber: 4-8g | Potassium: 400-800mg

Barley and Mushroom Stew

Yield: 4 servings | Prep time: 10 minutes | Cook time: 30 minutes

Ingredients:
- 1 tablespoon olive oil
- 1 onion, diced
- 2 cloves garlic, minced
- 8 ounces mushrooms, sliced (any variety you prefer)
- 1 cup pearl barley
- 4 cups vegetable broth
- 2 carrots, diced
- 2 celery stalks, diced
- Salt and pepper to taste
- Optional garnish: chopped fresh parsley

Directions:
1. In a large pot, heat olive oil over medium heat. Add diced onion and minced garlic, sauté until softened, about 5 minutes.
2. Add sliced mushrooms to the pot and cook until they release their moisture and start to brown, about 8-10 minutes.
3. Stir in pearl barley, vegetable broth, diced carrots, and diced celery. Bring to a simmer, then reduce heat to low, cover, and let simmer for about 20 minutes, or until barley and vegetables are tender.
4. Season with salt and pepper to taste. Serve hot, garnished with chopped fresh parsley if desired.

Nutritional Information (approximate per serving):
Calories: 200-350kcal | Protein: 6-12g | Carbohydrates: 30-60g | Fat: 5-10g | Cholesterol: 0mg | Sodium: 600-1200mg | Fiber: 6-12g | Potassium: 400-800mg

Lemon Cucumber Soup with Cilantro, Olives, and Capers

Yield: 4 servings | Prep time: 10 minutes | Cook time: 15 minutes

Ingredients:
- 2 cucumbers, peeled and chopped
- 1 lemon, juiced and zested
- 1/4 cup chopped fresh cilantro
- 1/4 cup sliced Kalamata olives
- 2 tablespoons capers
- 2 cloves garlic, minced
- 4 cups vegetable broth
- Salt and pepper, to taste
- Optional: Greek yogurt for garnish

Directions:
1. In a large pot, combine chopped cucumbers, lemon juice, lemon zest, chopped cilantro, sliced olives, capers, minced garlic, and vegetable broth.
2. Bring the mixture to a boil, then reduce heat and let it simmer for 10-12 minutes until the cucumbers are tender.
3. Using an immersion blender or regular blender, blend the soup until smooth.
4. Season with salt and pepper to taste.
5. Serve hot, garnished with a dollop of Greek yogurt if desired.

Nutritional Information (approximate):
Calories: 90kcal | Protein: 2g | Carbohydrates: 12g | Fat: 4g | Cholesterol: 0mg | Sodium: 780mg | Fiber: 3g | Potassium: 400mg

Cabbage Soup with Beans and Tomatoes

Yield: 4 servings | Prep time: 15 minutes | Cook time: 25 minutes

Ingredients:
- 1 tablespoon olive oil
- 1 onion, chopped
- 2 cloves garlic, minced
- 4 cups shredded cabbage
- 1 can (15 oz) diced tomatoes
- 2 cups vegetable broth
- 1 can (15 oz) kidney beans, drained and rinsed
- 1 teaspoon dried thyme
- Salt and pepper, to taste
- Fresh parsley, chopped, for garnish

Directions:
1. In a large pot, heat olive oil over medium heat. Add chopped onion and minced garlic, sauté until softened.
2. Add shredded cabbage to the pot and cook until slightly wilted, about 5 minutes.
3. Stir in diced tomatoes, vegetable broth, kidney beans, and dried thyme. Season with salt and pepper.
4. Bring the soup to a simmer, then reduce heat to low and let it cook for about 15-20 minutes, until the cabbage is tender.
5. Adjust seasoning if needed. Serve hot, garnished with fresh parsley.

Nutritional Information (approximate per serving):
Calories: 180kcal | Protein: 7g | Carbohydrates: 28g | Fat: 4g | Cholesterol: 0mg | Sodium: 560mg | Fiber: 8g | Potassium: 650mg

White Garlic Bean Soup

Yield: 4 servings | Prep time: 10 minutes | Cook time: 25 minutes

Ingredients:
- 2 tablespoons olive oil
- 4 cloves garlic, minced
- 2 cans (15 oz each) white beans, drained and rinsed
- 4 cups vegetable broth
- 1 teaspoon dried thyme
- Salt and pepper, to taste
- Fresh parsley, chopped, for garnish

Directions:
1. In a large pot, heat olive oil over medium heat. Add minced garlic and sauté until fragrant, about 1 minute.
2. Add white beans to the pot and stir to combine with garlic.
3. Pour in vegetable broth and add dried thyme. Bring to a simmer.
4. Reduce heat to low and let the soup simmer for about 20 minutes to allow flavors to meld together.
5. Season with salt and pepper to taste. Serve hot, garnished with fresh parsley.

Nutritional Information (approximate):
Calories: 220kcal | Protein: 10g | Carbohydrates: 32g | Fat: 6g | Cholesterol: 0mg | Sodium: 780mg | Fiber: 10g | Potassium: 640mg

Artichoke Soup with Spinach and Lemon

Yield: 4 servings | Prep time: 10 minutes | Cook time: 20 minutes

Ingredients:
- 2 tablespoons olive oil
- 1 onion, chopped
- 2 cloves garlic, minced
- 2 cans (14 oz each) artichoke hearts, drained and chopped
- 4 cups vegetable broth
- 2 cups fresh spinach leaves
- 1 lemon, juiced and zested
- Salt and pepper, to taste

Directions:
1. In a large pot, heat olive oil over medium heat. Add chopped onion and minced garlic, sauté until softened.

2. Add chopped artichoke hearts to the pot and cook for 2-3 minutes.
3. Pour in vegetable broth and bring to a simmer. Let it cook for about 10 minutes.
4. Stir in fresh spinach leaves and let them wilt in the soup.
5. Remove the pot from heat and stir in lemon juice and zest. Season with salt and pepper to taste.
6. Using an immersion blender or regular blender, blend the soup until smooth.
7. Serve hot, garnished with additional lemon zest if desired.

Nutritional Information (approximate per serving):
Calories: 180kcal | Protein: 5g | Carbohydrates: 20g | Fat: 10g | Cholesterol: 0mg | Sodium: 780mg | Fiber: 8g | Potassium: 480mg

White Bean Puree Soup with Pumpkin and Ginger

Yield: 4 servings | Prep time: 10 minutes | Cook time: 20 minutes

Ingredients:
- 1 can (15 oz) white beans, drained and rinsed
- 1 cup pumpkin puree
- 1 small onion, chopped
- 2 cloves garlic, minced
- 1 tablespoon fresh ginger, grated
- 4 cups vegetable broth
- Salt and pepper to taste
- Olive oil for sautéing
- Optional garnish: chopped parsley, pumpkin seeds

Directions:
1. In a large pot, heat olive oil over medium heat. Add chopped onions and sauté until translucent.
2. Add minced garlic and grated ginger, sauté for another minute until fragrant.
3. Stir in white beans, pumpkin puree, and vegetable broth. Bring to a simmer and cook for about 10-15 minutes.
4. Use an immersion blender or transfer the soup to a blender in batches to puree until smooth. Season with salt and pepper to taste.
5. Serve hot, garnished with chopped parsley and pumpkin seeds if desired.

Nutritional information (approximate):
Calories: 180kcal | Protein: 9g | Carbohydrates: 30g | Fat: 3g | Cholesterol: 0mg | Sodium: 650mg | Fiber: 8g | Potassium: 680mg

Oat Soup with Vegetables and Shrimp

Yield: 4 servings | Prep time: 15 minutes | Cook time: 25 minutes

Ingredients:
- 1 cup rolled oats
- 1 tablespoon olive oil
- 1 small onion, finely chopped
- 2 cloves garlic, minced
- 2 carrots, diced
- 2 celery stalks, diced
- 4 cups vegetable broth
- 12 oz shrimp, peeled and deveined
- Salt and pepper to taste
- Optional garnish: chopped parsley, lemon wedges

Directions:
1. Heat olive oil in a large pot over medium heat. Add chopped onions and sauté until translucent.
2. Add minced garlic, diced carrots, and diced celery. Sauté for about 5 minutes until vegetables are tender.
3. Stir in rolled oats and vegetable broth. Bring to a simmer and cook for 10-15 minutes until oats are cooked and soup has thickened.
4. Add shrimp to the pot and cook for another 5-7 minutes until shrimp are pink and cooked through.
5. Season with salt and pepper to taste. Serve hot, garnished with chopped parsley and lemon wedges if desired.

Nutritional information (approximate per serving):
Calories: 250kcal | Protein: 18g | Carbohydrates: 30g | Fat: 7g | Cholesterol: 115mg | Sodium: 800mg | Fiber: 5g | Potassium: 540mg

Cauliflower Soup with Broccoli and Potato

Yield: 4 servings | Prep time: 10 minutes | Cook time: 25 minutes

Ingredients:
- 1 small head cauliflower, chopped
- 1 cup broccoli florets
- 1 large potato, peeled and diced
- 1 small onion, chopped
- 2 cloves garlic, minced
- 4 cups vegetable broth
- Salt and pepper to taste
- Olive oil for sautéing
- Optional garnish: chopped chives, grated cheese

Directions:
1. In a large pot, heat olive oil over medium heat. Add chopped onions and sauté until translucent.
2. Add minced garlic and cook for another minute until fragrant.
3. Add diced potato, cauliflower, broccoli, and vegetable broth to the pot. Bring to a boil, then reduce heat and simmer for about 15-20 minutes until vegetables are tender.
4. Use an immersion blender or transfer the soup to a blender in batches to puree until smooth. Season with salt and pepper to taste.
5. Serve hot, garnished with chopped chives and grated cheese if desired.

Nutritional information (approximate per serving):
Calories: 150kcal | Protein: 5g | Carbohydrates: 25g | Fat: 4g | Cholesterol: 0mg | Sodium: 800mg | Fiber: 6g | Potassium: 750mg

Chicken Broth Curry Soup with Vegetables

Yield: 4 servings | Prep time: 15 minutes | Cook time: 20 minutes

Ingredients:
- 4 cups chicken broth
- 1 cup mixed vegetables (carrots, peas, bell peppers, etc.), diced
- 1 small onion, chopped
- 2 cloves garlic, minced
- 1 teaspoon curry powder
- 1 teaspoon turmeric powder
- Salt and pepper to taste
- 1 tablespoon olive oil
- Cooked chicken breast, shredded (optional)
- Fresh cilantro for garnish (optional)

Directions:
1. Heat olive oil in a large pot over medium heat. Add chopped onions and sauté until translucent.
2. Add minced garlic, curry powder, and turmeric powder. Cook for another minute until fragrant.
3. Pour in chicken broth and bring to a simmer. Add mixed vegetables and cook for about 10-15 minutes until vegetables are tender.
4. If using, add shredded chicken breast to the soup and heat through.
5. Season with salt and pepper to taste. Serve hot, garnished with fresh cilantro if desired.

Nutritional information (approximate per serving):
Calories: 120kcal | Protein: 8g | Carbohydrates: 10g | Fat: 5g | Cholesterol: 5mg | Sodium: 800mg | Fiber: 3g | Potassium: 500mg

Tomato Cocktail Soup with Shrimp and Avocado

Yield: 4 servings | Prep time: 10 minutes | Cook time: 15 minutes

Ingredients:
- 4 cups tomato juice
- 1 avocado, diced
- 12 oz shrimp, peeled and deveined
- 1 small onion, finely chopped
- 2 cloves garlic, minced
- 1 tablespoon olive oil
- Salt and pepper to taste
- Optional garnish: chopped cilantro, lime wedges

Directions:
1. In a large pot, heat olive oil over medium heat. Add chopped onions and sauté until translucent.
2. Add minced garlic and cook for another minute until fragrant.
3. Pour in tomato juice and bring to a simmer. Add shrimp and cook for about 5-7 minutes until shrimp are pink and cooked through.
4. Stir in diced avocado and cook for another minute until heated through.
5. Season with salt and pepper to taste. Serve hot, garnished with chopped cilantro and lime wedges if desired.

Nutritional information (approximate per serving):
Calories: 220kcal | Protein: 18g | Carbohydrates: 15g | Fat: 10g | Cholesterol: 150mg | Sodium: 600mg | Fiber: 5g | Potassium: 750mg

Onion Soup with Potato and Carrot

Yield: 4 servings | Prep time: 10 minutes | Cook time: 25 minutes

Ingredients:
- 2 large onions, thinly sliced
- 1 large potato, peeled and diced
- 2 carrots, diced
- 2 cloves garlic, minced
- 4 cups vegetable broth
- 1 tablespoon olive oil
- Salt and pepper to taste
- Optional garnish: chopped chives, grated cheese

Directions:
1. In a large pot, heat olive oil over medium heat. Add thinly sliced onions and cook until caramelized, stirring occasionally, about 15-20 minutes.
2. Add minced garlic and cook for another minute until fragrant.
3. Stir in diced potato, diced carrots, and vegetable broth. Bring to a boil, then reduce heat and simmer for about 10-15 minutes until vegetables are tender.
4. Use an immersion blender or transfer the soup to a blender in batches to puree until smooth. Alternatively, you can leave the soup chunky if desired.
5. Season with salt and pepper to taste. Serve hot, garnished with chopped chives and grated cheese if desired.

Nutritional information (approximate per serving):
Calories: 180kcal | Protein: 4g | Carbohydrates: 30g | Fat: 5g | Cholesterol: 0mg | Sodium: 800mg | Fiber: 6g | Potassium: 700mg

Sauces

Avocado Cilantro Lime Sauce

Yield: 4 servings | Prep time: 10 minutes | Cook time: 0 minutes

---

Ingredients:
- 1 ripe avocado, peeled and pitted
- 1/4 cup fresh cilantro leaves, chopped
- 1 lime, juiced
- 1/4 cup Greek yogurt
- 1 clove garlic, minced
- Salt and pepper to taste

Directions:
1. In a blender or food processor, combine the avocado, cilantro, lime juice, Greek yogurt, and minced garlic.
2. Blend until smooth and creamy, scraping down the sides as needed.
3. Season with salt and pepper to taste. Adjust lime juice or yogurt for desired consistency.
4. Transfer the sauce to a serving bowl. Serve immediately or refrigerate until ready to use.

Nutritional information (approximate per serving):
Calories: 85kcal | Protein: 2g | Carbohydrates: 6g | Fat: 7g | Cholesterol: 0mg | Sodium: 6mg | Fiber: 3g | Potassium: 281mg

Basil Pesto with Walnuts

Yield: 4 servings | Prep time: 15 minutes | Cook time: 0 minutes

---

Ingredients:
- 2 cups fresh basil leaves, packed
- 1/2 cup walnuts
- 1/2 cup grated Parmesan cheese
- 1/2 cup extra virgin olive oil
- 3 cloves garlic
- Salt and pepper to taste

Directions:
1. In a food processor, combine the basil leaves, walnuts, Parmesan cheese, and garlic cloves.
2. Pulse until the ingredients are finely chopped.
3. While the food processor is running, slowly pour in the olive oil until the mixture forms a smooth paste.
4. Season with salt and pepper to taste. Adjust consistency with more olive oil if needed.
5. Transfer the pesto to a serving bowl. Serve immediately or store in an airtight container in the refrigerator.

Nutritional information (approximate per serving):
Calories: 268kcal | Protein: 5g | Carbohydrates: 2g | Fat: 28g | Cholesterol: 7mg | Sodium: 168mg | Fiber: 1g | Potassium: 114mg

Peanut Ginger Sauce

Yield: 4 servings | Prep time: 10 minutes Cook time: 5 minutes

---

Ingredients:
- 1/2 cup creamy peanut butter
- 2 tablespoons soy sauce
- 2 tablespoons rice vinegar
- 1 tablespoon honey
- 1 tablespoon freshly grated ginger
- 1 clove garlic, minced
- 1/4 cup water
- Optional: Sriracha or hot sauce to taste

Directions:
1. In a small saucepan, combine the peanut butter, soy sauce, rice vinegar, honey, grated ginger, minced garlic, and water.
2. Cook over low heat, stirring constantly, until the sauce is smooth and heated through, about 5 minutes.
3. If desired, add Sriracha or hot sauce to taste for added spice.
4. Remove from heat and let cool slightly before serving.
5. Serve the peanut ginger sauce as a dipping sauce for spring rolls, drizzle over grilled chicken or tofu, or use as a dressing for salads.

Nutritional information (approximate):
Calories: 194kcal | Protein: 7g | Carbohydrates: 11g | Fat: 15g | Cholesterol: 0mg | Sodium: 415mg | Fiber: 2g | Potassium: 195mg

Tomato and Roasted Red Pepper Sauce

Yield: 4 servings | Prep time: 10 minutes | Cook time: 20 minutes

Ingredients:
- 1 can (14.5 oz) diced tomatoes
- 1 cup roasted red peppers, drained and chopped
- 2 cloves garlic, minced
- 1 tablespoon olive oil
- 1 teaspoon dried oregano
- Salt and pepper to taste
- Optional: red pepper flakes for heat

Directions:
1. In a saucepan, heat the olive oil over medium heat. Add the minced garlic and cook until fragrant, about 1 minute.
2. Add the diced tomatoes, roasted red peppers, dried oregano, salt, and pepper to the saucepan. Stir to combine.
3. Bring the mixture to a simmer, then reduce the heat to low. Let the sauce simmer gently for about 15 minutes, stirring occasionally, until it thickens slightly.
4. Taste and adjust seasoning as needed. If you like it spicy, add red pepper flakes to taste.
5. Once the sauce is ready, remove from heat and let it cool slightly before serving.

Nutritional information (approximate):
Calories: 53kcal | Protein: 1g | Carbohydrates: 6g | Fat: 3g | Cholesterol: 0mg | Sodium: 396mg | Fiber: 2g | Potassium: 233mg

Golden Turmeric Tahini Sauce

Yield: 4 servings | Prep time: 5 minutes | Cook time: 5 minutes

Ingredients:
- 1/4 cup tahini
- 1/4 cup water
- 2 tablespoons lemon juice
- 1 tablespoon olive oil
- 1 teaspoon ground turmeric
- 1/2 teaspoon ground cumin
- 1/4 teaspoon garlic powder
- Salt to taste

Directions:
1. In a small bowl, whisk together the tahini, water, lemon juice, and olive oil until smooth.
2. Stir in the ground turmeric, ground cumin, garlic powder, and salt until well combined.
3. If the sauce is too thick, add more water, a tablespoon at a time, until desired consistency is reached.
4. Taste and adjust seasoning as needed, adding more salt or lemon juice if desired.
5. Serve the golden turmeric tahini sauce immediately or refrigerate in an airtight container until ready to use.

Nutritional information (approximate):
Calories: 108kcal | Protein: 2g | Carbohydrates: 4g | Fat: 10g | Cholesterol: 0mg | Sodium: 69mg | Fiber: 1g | Potassium: 91mg

Mango Avocado Salsa

Yield: 4 servings | Prep time: 15 minutes | Cook time: 0 minutes

Ingredients:
- 1 ripe mango, diced
- 1 ripe avocado, diced
- 1/4 cup red onion, finely chopped
- 1/4 cup fresh cilantro, chopped
- Juice of 1 lime
- Salt and pepper to taste

Directions:
1. In a medium bowl, combine the diced mango, diced avocado, chopped red onion, and chopped cilantro.
2. Squeeze the lime juice over the salsa.

3. Season with salt and pepper to taste. Stir gently to combine.

Nutritional Information (approximate per serving):
Calories: 80-150kcal | Protein: 1-3g | Carbohydrates: 10-20g | Fat: 4-8g | Cholesterol: 0-5mg | Sodium: 0-100mg | Fiber: 3-5g | Potassium: 250-400mg

Lemon Ginger Sauce

Yield: 4 servings | Prep time: 5 minutes | Cook time: 5 minutes

Ingredients:
- 1/4 cup lemon juice
- 2 tablespoons honey
- 1 tablespoon grated ginger
- 1 teaspoon soy sauce
- 1 teaspoon cornstarch
- 2 tablespoons water

Directions:
1. In a small saucepan, combine the lemon juice, honey, grated ginger, and soy sauce.
2. In a small bowl, mix the corn-starch with water until dissolved, then add it to the saucepan.
3. Cook the mixture over medium heat, stirring constantly, until it thickens to desired consistency, about 3-5 minutes.
4. Remove from heat and let cool slightly before serving.

Nutritional Information (approximate per serving):
Calories: 30-60kcal | Protein: 0-1g | Carbohydrates: 8-12g | Fat: 0-1g | Cholesterol: 0mg | Sodium: 50-100mg | Fiber: 0-1g | Potassium: 20-40mg

Low-fat Horseradish Sauce

Yield: 4 servings | Prep time: 5 minutes | Cook time: 0 minutes

Ingredients:
- 1/2 cup low-fat Greek yogurt
- 2 tablespoons prepared horseradish
- 1 tablespoon Dijon mustard
- 1 tablespoon lemon juice
- Salt and pepper to taste

Directions:
1. In a small bowl, combine the low-fat Greek yogurt, prepared horseradish, Dijon mustard, and lemon juice.
2. Season with salt and pepper to taste.
3. Stir until well combined.

Nutritional Information (approximate per serving):
Calories: 20-40kcal | Protein: 2-4g | Carbohydrates: 2-4g | Fat: 0-1g | Cholesterol: 0-5mg | Sodium: 50-100mg | Fiber: 0g | Potassium: 50-100mg

Chimichurri Sauce

Yield: 4 servings | Prep time: 10 minutes | Cook time: 0 minutes

Ingredients:
- 1 cup fresh parsley, finely chopped
- 1/4 cup fresh cilantro, finely chopped
- 3 cloves garlic, minced
- 2 tablespoons red wine vinegar
- 1/2 teaspoon red pepper flakes (optional)
- 1/2 cup extra virgin olive oil
- Salt and pepper to taste

Directions:
1. In a medium bowl, combine the finely chopped parsley, finely chopped cilantro, minced garlic, red wine vinegar, and red pepper flakes (if using).
2. Gradually whisk in the extra virgin olive oil until well combined and emulsified.
3. Season with salt and pepper to taste. Adjust seasoning if needed.

Nutritional Information (approximate per serving):
Calories: 160-270kcal | Protein: 1-2g | Carbohydrates: 2-4g | Fat: 18-25g | Cholesterol: 0mg | Sodium: 0-100mg | Fiber: 1-2g | Potassium: 100-200mg

Blueberry Lemon Sauce

Yield: 4 servings | Prep time: 5 minutes | Cook time: 10 minutes

Ingredients:
- 1 cup blueberries
- 1/4 cup sugar
- Zest and juice of 1 lemon
- 1/4 cup water
- 1 teaspoon corn-starch

Directions:
1. In a saucepan, combine the blueberries, sugar, lemon zest, lemon juice, and water.
2. Bring the mixture to a simmer over medium heat, stirring occasionally.
3. In a small bowl, mix the corn starch with a tablespoon of water until smooth. Add the corn starch mixture to the saucepan and stir well.
4. Continue to simmer for 5-7 minutes, or until the sauce has thickened and the blueberries have softened.
5. Remove from heat and let cool slightly before serving.

Nutritional Information (approximate per serving):
Calories: 50-100kcal | Protein: 0-1g | Carbohydrates: 12-18g | Fat: 0-1g | Cholesterol: 0mg | Sodium: 0-10mg | Fiber: 1-2g | Potassium: 50-100mg

Creamy Dill Sauce

Yield: 4 servings | Prep time: 5 minutes | Cook time: 0 minutes

Ingredients:
- 1/2 cup sour cream
- 2 tablespoons mayonnaise
- 1 tablespoon fresh dill, chopped
- 1 tablespoon lemon juice
- Salt and pepper to taste

Directions:
1. In a small bowl, mix together the sour cream and mayonnaise until smooth.
2. Stir in the chopped fresh dill and lemon juice.
3. Season with salt and pepper to taste. Adjust seasoning if needed.
4. Serve immediately or refrigerate until ready to use.

Nutritional Information (approximate per serving):
Calories: 50-100kcal | Protein: 0-1g | Carbohydrates: 1-2g | Fat: 5-10g | Cholesterol: 5-10mg | Sodium: 50-100mg | Fiber: 0g | Potassium: 20-40mg

Spicy Mustard Sauce

Yield: 4 servings | Prep time: 5 minutes | Cook time: 0 minutes

Ingredients:
- 1/2 cup mayonnaise
- 2 tablespoons Dijon mustard
- 1 tablespoon honey
- 1 teaspoon hot sauce (adjust to taste)
- 1 tablespoon apple cider vinegar
- Salt and pepper to taste

Directions:
1. In a small bowl, whisk together the mayonnaise, Dijon mustard, honey, hot sauce, and apple cider vinegar until smooth.
2. Taste and adjust the level of spiciness by adding more hot sauce if desired.
3. Season with salt and pepper to taste.
4. Serve immediately or refrigerate until ready to use.

Nutritional Information (per serving):
Calories: 100-200kcal | Protein: 0-1g | Carbohydrates: 3-5g | Fat: 10-20g | Cholesterol: 5-10mg | Sodium: 150-300mg | Fiber: 0g | Potassium: 20-40mg

Roasted Garlic Sauce

Yield: 4 servings | Prep time: 5 minutes | Cook time: 30 minutes

Ingredients
- 1 bulb garlic
- 2 tablespoons olive oil
- 1/2 cup vegetable broth
- 1/4 cup heavy cream
- Salt and pepper to taste

Directions:
1. Preheat the oven to 400°F (200°C).
2. Slice off the top of the garlic bulb to expose the cloves, drizzle with olive oil, and wrap it in foil.
3. Roast the garlic in the oven for about 30 minutes, or until soft and caramelized.
4. Squeeze the roasted garlic cloves into a small saucepan, discarding the papery skins.
5. Add vegetable broth and heavy cream to the saucepan. Bring to a simmer over medium heat, stirring occasionally, until the sauce thickens slightly.
6. Season with salt and pepper to taste.

Nutritional Information (approximate per serving):
Calories: 100-200kcal | Protein: 1-2g | Carbohydrates: 3-5g | Fat: 9-12g | Cholesterol: 5-10mg | Sodium: 100-200mg | Fiber: 0-1g | Potassium: 100-200mg

Cucumber Dill Yogurt Sauce

Yield: 4 servings | Prep time: 10 minutes | Cook time: 0 minutes

Ingredients:
- 1 cup Greek yogurt
- 1/2 cucumber, grated
- 2 tablespoons fresh dill, chopped
- 1 tablespoon lemon juice
- Salt and pepper to taste

Directions:
1. In a small bowl, combine the Greek yogurt, grated cucumber, chopped fresh dill, and lemon juice.
2. Stir until well mixed.
3. Season with salt and pepper to taste. Adjust seasoning if needed.
4. Serve immediately or refrigerate until ready to use.

Nutritional Information (approximate per serving):
Calories: 30-60kcal | Protein: 3-5g | Carbohydrates: 2-4g | Fat: 1-2g | Cholesterol: 5-10mg | Sodium: 20-40mg | Fiber: 0-1g | Potassium: 100-150mg

Main course

Meat

Oven-Roasted Turkey Breast

Yield: 4 servings | Prep Time: 15 minutes | Cook Time: 90 minutes

Ingredients:
- 1 bone-in turkey breast (about 3 pounds)
- 2 tablespoons olive oil
- 1 teaspoon dried thyme
- 1 teaspoon dried rosemary
- 1/2 teaspoon garlic powder

- Salt and black pepper to taste
- 1 lemon, cut into wedges (for roasting)

Directions:
1. Preheat the oven to 350°F. Pat the turkey breast dries with paper towels.
2. Mix olive oil, thyme, rosemary, garlic powder, salt, and pepper in a small bowl. Rub the mixture all over the turkey breast.
3. Place the turkey breast on a rack in a roasting pan. Surround with lemon wedges.
4. Roast in the preheated oven for approximately 90 minutes or until an internal thermometer register 165°F.
5. Let the turkey rest for 10-15 minutes before slicing.

Nutritional Information per serving (approximate):
Calories: 300kcal | Protein: 53g | Carbohydrates: 0g | Fat: 7g | Cholesterol: 125mg | Sodium: 110mg | Fiber: 0g | Potassium: 500mg

Chicken Kebabs with Vegetables

Yield: 4 servings | Prep time: 15 minutes | Cook time: 15 minutes

Ingredients:
- 1 lb boneless, skinless chicken breasts, cut into chunks
- 1 bell pepper, cut into chunks
- 1 zucchini, sliced
- 1 red onion, cut into chunks
- 8 cherry tomatoes
- 2 tablespoons olive oil
- 2 cloves garlic, minced
- 1 teaspoon dried oregano
- 1 teaspoon paprika
- Salt and pepper, to taste
- Wooden or metal skewers

Directions:
1. If using wooden skewers, soak them in water for 30 minutes to prevent burning.
2. In a bowl, combine the chicken chunks, bell pepper, zucchini, red onion, and cherry tomatoes.
3. In a small bowl, mix the olive oil, minced garlic, dried oregano, paprika, salt, and pepper. Pour this marinade over the chicken and vegetables and toss to coat evenly.
4. Thread the marinated chicken and vegetables onto skewers, alternating between ingredients.
5. Preheat a grill or grill pan over medium-high heat. Grill the kebabs for about 12-15 minutes, turning occasionally, until the chicken is cooked through, and the vegetables are tender and lightly charred.
6. Serve the chicken kebabs hot, with your choice of side dishes.

Nutritional information (approximate):
Calories: 267kcal | Protein: 28g | Carbohydrates: 8g | Fat: 14g | Cholesterol: 73mg | Sodium: 73mg | Fiber: 2g | Potassium: 615mg

Grilled Lemon Herb Chicken Breast

Yield: 4 servings | Prep Time: 35 minutes (includes marinating time) | Cook Time: 12 minutes

Ingredients:
- 4 boneless, skinless chicken breasts (about 1 1/2 pounds)
- 2 tablespoons olive oil
- Juice of 1 lemon
- 2 garlic cloves, minced
- 1 teaspoon dried oregano
- 1 teaspoon dried thyme
- 1 teaspoon dried rosemary
- Salt and freshly ground black pepper, to taste
- Lemon slices and fresh herbs for garnish

Directions:
1. In a bowl, whisk together olive oil, lemon juice, garlic, oregano, thyme, rosemary, salt, and pepper.
2. Place chicken breasts in a resealable plastic bag and pour the marinade over them. Seal and refrigerate for at least 30 minutes to marinate.
3. Preheat the grill to medium-high heat. Remove chicken from the marinade and grill for about 5-6 minutes per side or until the internal temperature reaches 165°F.

4. Let the chicken rest for a few minutes before slicing. Serve with lemon slices and a garnish of fresh herbs.

Nutritional Information per serving (approximate):
Calories: 230kcal | Protein: 35g | Carbohydrates: 2g | Fat: 9g | Cholesterol: 95mg | Sodium: 70mg | Fiber: 0g | Potassium: 370mg

Baked Beef Steak with Herbs

Yield: 4 servings | Prep time: 10 minutes | Cook time: 20 minutes

Ingredients:
- 4 beef steaks (about 6 oz each), such as sirloin or ribeye
- 2 tablespoons olive oil
- 2 cloves garlic, minced
- 1 teaspoon dried thyme
- 1 teaspoon dried rosemary
- Salt and pepper to taste

Directions:
1. Preheat the oven to 400°F (200°C).
2. In a small bowl, mix olive oil, minced garlic, dried thyme, dried rosemary, salt, and pepper.
3. Place the beef steaks on a baking sheet lined with parchment paper.
4. Brush the olive oil mixture over the steaks, coating them evenly.
5. Bake in the preheated oven for about 15-20 minutes, depending on desired doneness.
6. Remove from the oven and let the steaks rest for a few minutes before serving.

Nutritional information (approximate per serving):
Calories: 350kcal | Protein: 40g | Carbohydrates: 0g | Fat: 20g | Cholesterol: 120mg | Sodium: 70mg | Fiber: 0g | Potassium: 600mg

Turkey Patties with Oats

Yield: 4 servings | Prep time: 10 minutes | Cook time: 15 minutes

Ingredients:
- 1 lb ground turkey
- 1/2 cup oats
- 1 small onion, finely chopped
- 2 cloves garlic, minced
- 1 teaspoon dried thyme
- Salt and pepper to taste

Directions:
1. In a mixing bowl, combine ground turkey, oats, chopped onion, minced garlic, dried thyme, salt, and pepper.
2. Mix until well combined, then shape the mixture into patties.
3. Heat a non-stick skillet over medium heat and lightly coat with cooking spray or oil.
4. Cook the turkey patties for about 6-7 minutes on each side, or until they are cooked through and golden brown.
5. Serve hot with your favorite side dishes or in a burger bun with toppings of your choice.

Nutritional information (approximate per serving):
Calories: 200kcal | Protein: 25g | Carbohydrates: 10g | Fat: 7g | Cholesterol: 60mg | Sodium: 300mg | Fiber: 2g | Potassium: 350mg

Stuffed Chicken Breasts with Spinach and Mushrooms

Yield: 4 servings | Prep time: 15 minutes | Cook time: 25 minutes

Ingredients:
- 4 boneless, skinless chicken breasts
- 1 cup fresh spinach, chopped
- 1 cup mushrooms, sliced
- 1/2 cup shredded mozzarella cheese
- 2 cloves garlic, minced
- Salt and pepper to taste

Directions:
1. Preheat the oven to 375°F (190°C).
2. In a skillet, sauté the mushrooms and garlic until softened. Add the chopped spinach and cook until wilted. Season with salt and pepper.

3. Butterfly each chicken breast by slicing horizontally, but not all the way through, so you can open it like a book.
4. Spoon the spinach and mushroom mixture onto one half of each chicken breast. Sprinkle with shredded mozzarella cheese, then fold the other half of the chicken breast over the filling.
5. Secure the stuffed chicken breasts with toothpicks if needed, then place them in a baking dish.
6. Bake in the preheated oven for about 20-25 minutes, or until the chicken is cooked through and no longer pink in the center.
7. Remove the toothpicks before serving.

Nutritional information (approximate per serving):
Calories: 250kcal | Protein: 40g | Carbohydrates: 4g | Fat: 8g | Cholesterol: 110mg | Sodium: 350mg | Fiber: 1g | Potassium: 550mg

Turmeric-Ginger Baked Chicken

Yield: 4 servings | Prep time: 10 minutes | Cook time: 25 minutes

Ingredients:
- 4 boneless, skinless chicken breasts
- 2 tablespoons olive oil
- 1 tablespoon ground turmeric
- 1 tablespoon grated fresh ginger
- 2 cloves garlic, minced
- 1 teaspoon ground cumin
- 1 teaspoon paprika
- Salt and pepper to taste
- Fresh cilantro for garnish (optional)

Directions:
1. Preheat the oven to 400°F (200°C). Place the chicken breasts in a baking dish.
2. In a small bowl, whisk together the olive oil, ground turmeric, grated ginger, minced garlic, ground cumin, paprika, salt, and pepper.
3. Pour the turmeric-ginger mixture over the chicken breasts, making sure they are evenly coated.
4. Bake in the preheated oven for 20-25 minutes, or until the chicken is cooked through and no longer pink in the center.
5. Garnish with fresh cilantro before serving, if desired.

Nutritional information (approximate per serving):
Calories: 250kcal | Protein: 28g | Carbohydrates: 2g | Fat: 14g | Cholesterol: 80mg | Sodium: 90mg | Fiber: 1g | Potassium: 480mg

Herb-Crusted Lamb Chops

Yield: 4 servings | Prep time: 15 minutes | Cook time: 15 minutes

Ingredients:
- 8 lamb loin chops, about 1 inch thick
- 2 tablespoons olive oil
- 2 cloves garlic, minced
- 2 tablespoons fresh rosemary, chopped
- 2 tablespoons fresh thyme leaves, chopped
- 1 teaspoon salt
- 1/2 teaspoon black pepper

Directions:
1. Preheat the oven to 400°F (200°C).
2. In a small bowl, mix the olive oil, minced garlic, chopped rosemary, chopped thyme, salt, and pepper.
3. Rub the herb mixture evenly over both sides of the lamb chops.
4. Heat a large oven-safe skillet over medium-high heat. Sear the lamb chops for 2 minutes on each side.
5. Transfer the skillet to the preheated oven and roast for 8-10 minutes for medium-rare or until desired doneness is reached.

Nutritional information (approximate per serving):
Calories: 380kcal | Protein: 30g | Carbohydrates: 2g | Fat: 28g | Cholesterol: 105mg | Sodium: 660mg | Fiber: 1g | Potassium: 410mg

Mediterranean Turkey Burgers

Yield: 4 servings | Prep time: 10 minutes | Cook time: 12 minutes

Ingredients:
- 1 lb ground turkey
- 1/4 cup finely chopped red onion
- 1/4 cup chopped sun-dried tomatoes
- 2 cloves garlic, minced
- 1/4 cup chopped fresh parsley
- 1 teaspoon dried oregano
- 1/2 teaspoon ground cumin
- Salt and black pepper to taste
- 4 hamburger buns
- Toppings: lettuce, tomato, cucumber, feta cheese (optional)

Directions:
1. In a large bowl, combine ground turkey, red onion, sun-dried tomatoes, minced garlic, chopped parsley, dried oregano, ground cumin, salt, and black pepper. Mix until well combined.
2. Divide the mixture into 4 equal portions and shape them into burger patties.
3. Preheat a grill or grill pan over medium-high heat. Cook the turkey burgers for about 5-6 minutes on each side or until cooked through.
4. Toast the hamburger buns on the grill for a minute or until lightly browned.
5. Serve the turkey burgers on the toasted buns with your choice of toppings.

Rosemary Chicken and Potatoes

Yield: 4 servings | Prep time: 15 minutes | Cook time: 40 minutes

Ingredients:
- 4 bone-in, skin-on chicken thighs
- 4 medium potatoes, diced
- 2 tablespoons olive oil
- 3 cloves garlic, minced
- 1 tablespoon fresh rosemary, chopped
- 1 teaspoon paprika
- Salt and black pepper to taste
- Fresh parsley for garnish (optional)

Directions:
1. Preheat the oven to 400°F (200°C).
2. In a large bowl, toss the diced potatoes with olive oil, minced garlic, chopped rosemary, paprika, salt, and black pepper until evenly coated.
3. Arrange the seasoned potatoes on a baking sheet in a single layer. Place the chicken thighs on top of the potatoes.
4. Roast in the preheated oven for about 35-40 minutes or until the chicken is cooked through and the potatoes are golden brown and tender.
5. Garnish with fresh parsley before serving, if desired.

Nutritional information (approximate per serving):
Calories: 380kcal | Protein: 22g | Carbohydrates: 25g | Fat: 22g | Cholesterol: 80mg | Sodium: 85mg | Fiber: 3g | Potassium: 850mg

Braised Turkey with Vegetables and Lentils

Yield: 4 servings | Prep time: 15 minutes | Cook time: 45 minutes

Ingredients:
- 1 lb turkey breast, cut into chunks
- 1 tablespoon olive oil
- 1 onion, chopped
- 2 carrots, diced
- 2 celery stalks, diced
- 3 cloves garlic, minced
- 1 cup dried lentils, rinsed
- 2 cups chicken or vegetable broth
- 1 teaspoon dried thyme
- Salt and pepper to taste

Directions:
1. Heat olive oil in a large skillet over medium heat. Add turkey chunks and brown on all sides, then remove from skillet and set aside.
2. In the same skillet, add onion, carrots, celery, and garlic. Sauté until vegetables are softened, about 5 minutes.
3. Return turkey to the skillet. Add lentils, broth, thyme, salt, and pepper. Bring to a simmer, then

cover and cook for 30 minutes, or until lentils are tender and turkey is cooked through.
4. Serve hot, garnished with fresh herbs if desired.

Nutritional Information (approximate per serving):
Calories: 320kcal | Protein: 28g | Carbohydrates: 28g | Fat: 10g | Cholesterol: 60mg | Sodium: 600mg | Fiber: 12g | Potassium: 800mg

Beef in its Own Juice with Zucchini and Pumpkin

Yield: 4 servings | Prep time: 10 minutes | Cook time: 40 minutes

Ingredients:
- 1 lb. beef stew meat, cut into chunks
- 2 zucchinis, sliced
- 1 small pumpkin, peeled, seeded, and diced
- 1 onion, chopped
- 3 cloves garlic, minced
- Salt and pepper to taste

Directions:
1. In a large skillet or pot, sear the beef chunks over medium-high heat until browned on all sides, about 5 minutes.
2. Add the chopped onion and minced garlic to the skillet with the beef. Cook until the onion is translucent, stirring occasionally, about 5 minutes.
3. Add the sliced zucchinis and diced pumpkin to the skillet. Season with salt and pepper. Cover and simmer over low heat for 30 minutes, or until the beef is tender and the vegetables are cooked through.
4. Serve hot, garnished with fresh herbs if desired.

Nutritional Information (approximate):
Calories: 290kcal | Protein: 30g | Carbohydrates: 15g | Fat: 12g | Cholesterol: 80mg | Sodium: 90mg | Fiber: 5g | Potassium: 800mg

Grilled Chicken with Avocado Salsa

- Yield: 4 servings Prep Time: 15 minutes
- Cook Time: 12 minutes

Ingredients:
- 4 boneless, skinless chicken breasts
- 2 ripe avocados, diced
- 1 tomato, diced
- 1/4 cup red onion, finely chopped
- 1/4 cup fresh cilantro, chopped
- Juice of 1 lime
- Salt and pepper to taste

Directions:
1. Preheat grill to medium-high heat. Season chicken breasts with salt and pepper.
2. Grill chicken breasts for about 6 minutes per side, or until cooked through and no longer pink in the center.
3. In a bowl, combine diced avocado, tomato, red onion, cilantro, lime juice, salt, and pepper to make the salsa.
4. Serve grilled chicken topped with avocado salsa.

Nutritional Information (approximate per serving):
Calories: 320kcal | Protein: 30g | Carbohydrates: 10g | Fat: 18g | Cholesterol: 80mg | Sodium: 450mg | Fiber: 6g | Potassium: 800mg

Turkey Chili with Beans and Vegetables

Yield: 4 servings | Prep time: 15 minutes | Cook time: 30 minutes

Ingredients
- 1 lb ground turkey
- 1 onion, diced
- 2 cloves garlic, minced
- 1 bell pepper, diced
- 1 zucchini, diced
- 1 can (15 oz) kidney beans, drained and rinsed
- 1 can (15 oz) diced tomatoes

- 1 cup chicken broth
- 2 tablespoons chili powder
- 1 teaspoon cumin
- Salt and pepper, to taste
- Optional toppings: shredded cheese, diced avocado, chopped cilantro

Directions:
1. In a large pot, cook ground turkey over medium heat until browned, breaking it apart with a spoon.
2. Add diced onion and minced garlic to the pot and cook for 2-3 minutes until softened.
3. Stir in diced bell pepper and zucchini, cooking for another 2-3 minutes.
4. Add kidney beans, diced tomatoes, chicken broth, chili powder, cumin, salt, and pepper to the pot. Bring to a simmer and let it cook for 20-25 minutes, stirring occasionally.
5. Taste and adjust seasoning as needed. Serve hot with optional toppings if desired.

Nutritional Information (approximate per serving):
Calories: 320kcal | Protein: 28g | Carbohydrates: 28g | Fat: 10g | Cholesterol: 65mg | Sodium: 780mg | Fiber: 8g | Potassium: 980mg

Baked Chicken Thighs with Rosemary and Garlic

Yield: 4 servings | Prep time: 10 minutes | Cook time: 35 minutes

Ingredients:
- 4 bone-in, skin-on chicken thighs
- 2 tablespoons olive oil
- 4 cloves garlic, minced
- 2 tablespoons fresh rosemary leaves, chopped
- Salt and pepper, to taste

Directions:
1. Preheat the oven to 400°F (200°C). Line a baking sheet with parchment paper or foil for easy cleanup.
2. In a small bowl, mix olive oil, minced garlic, and chopped rosemary.
3. Place chicken thighs on the prepared baking sheet. Season both sides with salt and pepper.
4. Brush the garlic and rosemary mixture over the chicken thighs, ensuring they are evenly coated.
5. Bake in the preheated oven for 30-35 minutes, or until the chicken is cooked through and golden brown on top.
6. Remove from the oven and let the chicken rest for a few minutes before serving.

Nutritional Information (approximate per serving):
Calories: 320kcal | Protein: 22g | Carbohydrates: 2g | Fat: 24g | Cholesterol: 110mg | Sodium: 240mg | Fiber: 0g | Potassium: 250mg

Beef Stir-Fry with Broccoli and Bell Peppers

Yield: 4 servings | Prep time: 15 minutes | Cook time: 10 minutes

Ingredients:
- 1 lb beef sirloin, thinly sliced
- 2 cups broccoli florets
- 1 red bell pepper, sliced
- 1 yellow bell pepper, sliced
- 3 cloves garlic, minced
- 2 tablespoons soy sauce
- 1 tablespoon oyster sauce
- 1 tablespoon sesame oil
- 1 teaspoon cornstarch
- 2 tablespoons vegetable oil, for cooking
- Salt and pepper, to taste
- Cooked rice, for serving

Directions:
1. In a small bowl, mix together soy sauce, oyster sauce, sesame oil, and cornstarch to make the sauce. Set aside.
2. Heat vegetable oil in a large skillet or wok over high heat. Add minced garlic and cook for 30 seconds until fragrant.
3. Add thinly sliced beef to the skillet and stir-fry for 2-3 minutes until browned.

4. Add broccoli florets and sliced bell peppers to the skillet. Stir-fry for another 3-4 minutes until the vegetables are tender-crisp.
5. Pour the sauce over the beef and vegetables, stirring well to coat everything evenly. Cook for an additional 1-2 minutes until the sauce thickens slightly.
6. Season with salt and pepper to taste. Serve hot over cooked rice.

Nutritional Information (approximate per serving):
Calories: 320kcal | Protein: 28g | Carbohydrates: 10g | Fat: 18g | Cholesterol: 70mg | Sodium: 580mg | Fiber: 3g | Potassium: 670mg

Roasted Chicken Quarters with Herbs and Root Vegetables

Yield: 4 servings | Prep time: 15 minutes | Cook time: 45 minutes

Ingredients:
- 4 chicken leg quarters
- 4 medium carrots, peeled and cut into chunks
- 2 medium potatoes, peeled and cut into chunks
- 1 onion, peeled and cut into wedges
- 4 cloves garlic, minced
- 2 tablespoons olive oil
- 1 tablespoon fresh rosemary, chopped
- 1 tablespoon fresh thyme leaves
- Salt and pepper, to taste

Directions:
1. Preheat the oven to 400°F (200°C). Line a baking sheet with parchment paper or foil.
2. In a small bowl, mix minced garlic, olive oil, chopped rosemary, and thyme leaves.
3. Place chicken leg quarters on the prepared baking sheet. Arrange carrots, potatoes, onion wedges around the chicken.
4. Brush the garlic and herb mixture over the chicken and vegetables, ensuring they are evenly coated. Season everything with salt and pepper.
5. Roast in the preheated oven for 40-45 minutes, or until the chicken is cooked through and the vegetables are tender.
6. Remove from the oven and let it rest for a few minutes before serving.

Nutritional Information (approximate per serving):
Calories: 380kcal | Protein: 28g | Carbohydrates: 20g | Fat: 22g | Cholesterol: 130mg | Sodium: 160mg | Fiber: 4g | Potassium: 840mg

Turkey Meatballs in Marinara Sauce over Zucchini Noodles

Yield: 4 servings | Prep time: 20 minutes | Cook time: 25 minutes

Ingredients:
- 1 lb. ground turkey
- 1/4 cup breadcrumbs (use almond meal for a gluten-free option)
- 1 egg
- 2 cloves garlic, minced
- 1/4 cup grated Parmesan cheese
- 2 tablespoons fresh parsley, chopped
- Salt and pepper, to taste
- 2 tablespoons olive oil
- 2 cups marinara sauce
- 4 medium zucchini, spiralized into noodles
- Fresh basil leaves, for garnish

Directions:
1. In a large bowl, mix ground turkey, breadcrumbs, egg, minced garlic, grated Parmesan cheese, chopped parsley, salt, and pepper until well combined. Form the mixture into meatballs, about 1 inch in diameter.
2. Heat olive oil in a large skillet over medium heat. Add the meatballs and cook for 5-6 minutes, turning occasionally, until browned on all sides.
3. Pour marinara sauce over the meatballs in the skillet. Reduce heat to low, cover, and simmer for 15-20 minutes, until the meatballs are cooked through.
4. While the meatballs are simmering, spiralize the zucchini into noodles using a spiralizer.

5. Heat a separate skillet over medium heat. Add the zucchini noodles and cook for 2-3 minutes until just tender.
6. Serve the turkey meatballs and marinara sauce over the zucchini noodles. Garnish with fresh basil leaves before serving.

Nutritional Information (approximate per serving):
Calories: 320kcal | Protein: 28g | Carbohydrates: 15g | Fat: 18g | Cholesterol: 95mg | Sodium: 680mg | Fiber: 4g | Potassium: 890mg

Herb-Roasted Lamb Leg with Mint Yogurt Sauce

Yield: 4 servings | Prep time: 15 minutes | Cook time: 1 hour

Ingredients:
- 1 (about 2 lb) boneless lamb leg
- 2 tablespoons olive oil
- 4 cloves garlic, minced
- 1 tablespoon fresh rosemary, chopped
- 1 tablespoon fresh thyme leaves
- Salt and pepper, to taste
- 1 cup Greek yogurt
- 2 tablespoons fresh mint leaves, chopped
- 1 tablespoon lemon juice

Directions:
1. Preheat the oven to 375°F (190°C).
2. In a small bowl, mix olive oil, minced garlic, chopped rosemary, and thyme leaves.
3. Place the lamb leg in a roasting pan. Rub the herb mixture all over the lamb, ensuring it is evenly coated. Season with salt and pepper.
4. Roast the lamb in the preheated oven for 50-60 minutes, or until cooked to your desired level of doneness.
5. While the lamb is roasting, prepare the mint yogurt sauce by combining Greek yogurt, chopped mint leaves, and lemon juice in a bowl. Stir well to combine.
6. Once the lamb is done, remove it from the oven and let it rest for a few minutes before slicing. Serve with the mint yogurt sauce on the side.

Nutritional Information (approximate per serving):
Calories: 380kcal | Protein: 40g | Carbohydrates: 4g | Fat: 22g | Cholesterol: 120mg | Sodium: 170mg | Fiber: 1g | Potassium: 540mg

Turkey Meatloaf with Zucchini

Yield: 4 servings | Prep time: 15 minutes | Cook time: 45 minutes

Ingredients:
- 1 lb (450g) ground turkey
- 1 cup grated zucchini
- 1/2 cup breadcrumbs
- 1/4 cup grated Parmesan cheese
- 1/4 cup chopped onion
- 1 egg, beaten
- 2 cloves garlic, minced
- 1/4 cup ketchup
- 1 tablespoon Worcestershire sauce
- 1 teaspoon dried oregano
- Salt and pepper to taste

Directions:
1. Preheat your oven to 375°F (190°C).
2. In a large mixing bowl, combine ground turkey, grated zucchini, breadcrumbs, Parmesan cheese, chopped onion, beaten egg, minced garlic, ketchup, Worcestershire sauce, dried oregano, salt, and pepper. Mix until well combined.
3. Shape the mixture into a loaf and place it in a greased loaf pan.
4. Bake in the preheated oven for about 45 minutes or until the meatloaf is cooked through and reaches an internal temperature of 165°F (74°C).
5. Let the meatloaf rest for a few minutes before slicing and serving.

Nutritional Information (approximate per serving):
Calories: 250kcal | Protein: 28g | Carbohydrates: 11g | Fat: 10g | Cholesterol: 105mg | Sodium: 450mg | Fiber: 2g | Potassium: 450mg

Balsamic Glazed Chicken Breast

Yield: 4 servings | Prep time: 10 minutes | Cook time: 20 minutes

Ingredients:
- 2-6 boneless, skinless chicken breasts
- Salt and pepper to taste
- 2 tablespoons olive oil
- 1/4 cup balsamic vinegar
- 2 tablespoons honey
- 2 cloves garlic, minced
- 1 teaspoon dried thyme

Directions:
1. Season chicken breasts with salt and pepper on both sides.
2. In a skillet over medium-high heat, heat olive oil. Add chicken breasts and cook until browned on both sides and cooked through, about 6-8 minutes per side.
3. In a small bowl, whisk together balsamic vinegar, honey, minced garlic, and dried thyme.
4. Pour the balsamic glaze over the cooked chicken breasts in the skillet. Allow it to simmer for a few minutes until the glaze thickens and coats the chicken evenly.
5. Serve the chicken breasts hot, drizzled with any remaining glaze from the skillet.

Nutritional Information (approximate per serving):
Calories: 250kcal | Protein: 30g | Carbohydrates: 10g | Fat: 10g | Cholesterol: 90mg | Sodium: 350mg | Fiber: 0g | Potassium: 400mg

Spiced Lean Pork Tenderloin

Yield: 4 servings | Prep time: 10 minutes | Cook time: 25minutes

Ingredients:
- 1-2 lbs (450-900g) pork tenderloin
- 1 teaspoon paprika
- 1 teaspoon garlic powder
- 1 teaspoon onion powder
- 1/2 teaspoon ground cumin
- 1/2 teaspoon ground coriander
- 1/2 teaspoon dried thyme
- Salt and pepper to taste
- 1 tablespoon olive oil

Directions:
1. Preheat the oven to 400°F (200°C).
2. In a small bowl, mix paprika, garlic powder, onion powder, ground cumin, ground coriander, dried thyme, salt, and pepper.
3. Rub the spice mixture evenly over the pork tenderloin.
4. In an oven-safe skillet, heat olive oil over medium-high heat. Sear the pork tenderloin on all sides until browned, about 2-3 minutes per side.
5. Transfer the skillet to the preheated oven and roast the pork tenderloin for about 20-25 minutes, or until the internal temperature reaches 145°F (63°C).
6. Remove the pork from the oven and let it rest for a few minutes before slicing and serving.

Nutritional Information (approximate per serving):
Calories: 200kcal | Protein: 25g | Carbohydrates: 2g | Fat: 9g | Cholesterol: 75mg | Sodium: 300mg | Fiber: 1g | Potassium: 400mg

Beef Stir-fry with Broccoli and Bell Pepper

Yield: 4 servings | Prep time: 15 minutes | Cook time: 15 minutes

Ingredients:
- 1 lb (450g) beef steak, thinly sliced
- 2 cups broccoli florets
- 1 bell pepper, sliced
- 2 tablespoons soy sauce
- 1 tablespoon oyster sauce
- 1 tablespoon sesame oil
- 2 cloves garlic, minced
- 1 teaspoon grated ginger
- 1 tablespoon cornstarch
- 2 tablespoons water
- Salt and pepper to taste
- 2 tablespoons vegetable oil for cooking

Directions:
1. In a small bowl, mix soy sauce, oyster sauce, sesame oil, minced garlic, grated ginger, cornstarch, and water to make the sauce. Set aside.
2. Heat vegetable oil in a large skillet or wok over high heat.
3. Add sliced beef to the skillet and stir-fry until browned, about 2-3 minutes.
4. Add broccoli florets and sliced bell pepper to the skillet. Continue to stir-fry for another 3-4 minutes, or until the vegetables are tender-crisp.
5. Pour the prepared sauce over the beef and vegetables in the skillet. Stir well to coat everything evenly with the sauce.
6. Cook for an additional 1-2 minutes, allowing the sauce to thicken slightly.
7. Remove from heat and serve the beef stir-fry hot over rice or noodles.

Nutritional Information (approximate per serving):
Calories: 250kcal | Protein: 25g | Carbohydrates: 10g | Fat: 12g | Cholesterol: 50mg | Sodium: 600mg | Fiber: 3g | Potassium: 550mg

Chicken Zucchini Skewers

Yield: 4 servings | Prep time: 20 minutes | Cook time: 10 minutes

Ingredients:
- 1 lb (450g) boneless, skinless chicken breasts, cut into chunks
- 2 medium zucchinis, sliced into rounds
- 2 tablespoons olive oil
- 2 cloves garlic, minced
- 1 teaspoon dried oregano
- 1 teaspoon dried thyme
- Salt and pepper to taste
- Wooden or metal skewers

Directions:
1. If using wooden skewers, soak them in water for at least 30 minutes to prevent burning.
2. In a small bowl, mix olive oil, minced garlic, dried oregano, dried thyme, salt, and pepper to create a marinade.
3. Thread alternating pieces of chicken and zucchini onto skewers.
4. Brush the marinade over the skewers, coating them evenly.
5. Preheat a grill or grill pan over medium-high heat. Grill the skewers for about 4-5 minutes on each side, or until the chicken is cooked through and the zucchini is tender.
6. Serve the chicken zucchini skewers hot, garnished with fresh herbs if desired.

Nutritional Information (approximate per serving):
Calories: 200kcal | Protein: 25g | Carbohydrates: 4g | Fat: 9g | Cholesterol: 70mg | Sodium: 300mg | Fiber: 1g | Potassium: 400mg

Lean Beef and Vegetable Kebabs

Yield: 4 servings | Prep time: 20 minutes | Cook time: 10 minutes

Ingredients:
- 1 lb (450g) lean beef, cut into cubes
- 2 bell peppers, cut into chunks
- 1 large onion, cut into chunks
- 8 oz (225g) mushrooms, halved
- 2 tablespoons olive oil
- 2 cloves garlic, minced
- 1 teaspoon dried rosemary
- 1 teaspoon dried thyme
- Salt and pepper to taste
- Wooden or metal skewers

Directions:
1. If using wooden skewers, soak them in water for at least 30 minutes to prevent burning.
2. In a small bowl, mix olive oil, minced garlic, dried rosemary, dried thyme, salt, and pepper to create a marinade.
3. Thread alternating pieces of beef, bell peppers, onions, and mushrooms onto skewers.
4. Brush the marinade over the kebabs, coating them evenly.
5. Preheat a grill or grill pan over medium-high heat. Grill the kebabs for about 4-5 minutes on each side, or until the beef is cooked to desired doneness and the vegetables are tender.
6. Serve the lean beef and vegetable kebabs hot, garnished with fresh herbs if desired.

Fish and Seafood

Baked Salmon with Green Vegetables

Yield: 4 servings | Prep time: 10 minutes | Cook time: 20 minutes

Ingredients:
- 4 salmon fillets (about 6 ounces each)
- 2 tablespoons olive oil
- 2 cloves garlic, minced
- 1 teaspoon dried dill
- Salt and pepper, to taste
- 2 cups green vegetables (such as asparagus, broccoli, or green beans), trimmed
- Lemon wedges, for serving

Directions:
1. Preheat the oven to 400°F (200°C). Line a baking sheet with parchment paper or foil.
2. Place the salmon fillets on the prepared baking sheet. Drizzle with olive oil and sprinkle minced garlic and dried dill over the top. Season with salt and pepper.
3. Arrange the green vegetables around the salmon on the baking sheet. Drizzle with a little more olive oil and season with salt and pepper.
4. Bake in the preheated oven for 15-20 minutes, or until the salmon is cooked through and flakes easily with a fork, and the vegetables are tender.
5. Serve the baked salmon and vegetables hot, with lemon wedges on the side for squeezing over the fish.

Nutritional Information (approximate per serving):
Calories: 250kcal | Protein: 30g | Carbohydrates: 8g | Fat: 10g | Cholesterol: 70mg | Sodium: 400mg | Fiber: 2g | Potassium: 500mg

Nutritional information (approximate per serving):
Calories: 342kcal | Protein: 34g | Carbohydrates: 6g | Fat: 20g | Cholesterol: 94mg | Sodium: 99mg | Fiber: 3g | Potassium: 849mg

Steamed Fish with Lemon and Herbs

Yield: 4 servings | Prep time: 10 minutes | Cook time: 15 minutes

Ingredients
- 4 fillets of white fish (such as cod or tilapia), about 6 oz each
- 1 lemon, thinly sliced
- 2 tablespoons fresh parsley, chopped
- 2 tablespoons fresh dill, chopped
- Salt and pepper to taste

Directions:
1. Prepare a steamer by filling a pot with water and bringing it to a boil. Place a steaming basket or rack in the pot.
2. Season the fish fillets with salt and pepper on both sides.
3. Arrange lemon slices on top of each fillet and sprinkle with chopped parsley and dill.
4. Once the water is boiling, place the fish fillets in the steaming basket, cover, and steam for about 10-12 minutes, or until the fish is cooked through and flakes easily with a fork.

5. Carefully remove the steamed fish from the basket and serve immediately, garnished with additional herbs if desired.

Nutritional information (approximate per serving):
Calories: 170kcal | Protein: 32g | Carbohydrates: 2g | Fat: 4g | Cholesterol: 85mg | Sodium: 100mg | Fiber: 1g | Potassium: 520mg

Baked Tuna Carpaccio

Yield: 4 servings | Prep time: 10 minutes | Cook time: 10 minutes

Ingredients:
- 1 lb tuna steaks
- 2 tablespoons olive oil
- 2 cloves garlic, minced
- 1 teaspoon dried oregano
- Salt and pepper to taste
- Lemon wedges, for serving
- Fresh parsley, chopped, for garnish

Directions:
1. Preheat the oven to 400°F (200°C).
2. Place the tuna steaks on a baking sheet lined with parchment paper.
3. In a small bowl, mix olive oil, minced garlic, dried oregano, salt, and pepper.
4. Brush the olive oil mixture over the tuna steaks, coating them evenly.
5. Bake in the preheated oven for about 8-10 minutes, or until the tuna is cooked through but still pink in the center.
6. Remove from the oven and let it rest for a few minutes.
7. Serve the baked tuna carpaccio with lemon wedges on the side for squeezing over the fish. Garnish with chopped fresh parsley.

Nutritional information (approximate per serving):
Calories: 250kcal | Protein: 30g | Carbohydrates: 1g | Fat: 14g | Cholesterol: 50mg | Sodium: 300mg | Fiber: 0g | Potassium: 400mg

Baked Salmon with Dill and Lemon

Yield: 4 servings | Prep Time: 10 minutes | Cook Time: 15 minutes

Ingredients:
- 4 salmon fillets (6 ounces each)
- 2 tablespoons fresh dill, chopped
- 1 lemon, thinly sliced
- 2 tablespoons olive oil
- Salt and pepper to taste

Directions:
1. Preheat the oven to 375°F. Line a baking sheet with parchment paper.
2. Place salmon fillets on the prepared baking sheet. Drizzle with olive oil and season with salt and pepper.
3. Top each fillet with lemon slices and sprinkle with fresh dill.
4. Bake in the preheated oven for about 12-15 minutes, or until salmon flakes easily with a fork.

Nutritional Information (approximate per serving):
 Calories: 300kcal | Protein: 23g | Carbohydrates: 0g | Fat: 22g | Cholesterol: 60mg | Sodium: 50mg | Fiber: 0g | Potassium: 500mg

Sautéed Shrimp with Garlic and Lemon

Yield: 4 servings | Prep time: 10 minutes | Cook time: 5 minutes

Ingredients:
- 1-pound large shrimp, peeled and deveined
- 3 tablespoons olive oil
- 4 cloves garlic, minced
- Zest of 1 lemon
- Juice of 1 lemon
- Salt and pepper to taste
- Fresh parsley for garnish (optional)

Directions:
1. In a large skillet, heat the olive oil over medium-high heat. Add the minced garlic and sauté for about 30 seconds, or until fragrant.
2. Add the shrimp to the skillet in a single layer. Cook for 2-3 minutes on each side, until they turn pink and opaque.
3. Stir in the lemon zest and lemon juice, tossing the shrimp to coat evenly. Season with salt and pepper to taste.
4. Remove the skillet from heat and transfer the shrimp to a serving platter. Garnish with fresh parsley, if desired, and serve immediately.

Nutritional information (approximate per serving):
Calories: 200kcal | Protein: 25g | Carbohydrates: 2g | Fat: 10g | Cholesterol: 230mg | Sodium: 240mg | Fiber: 0g | Potassium: 190mg

Grilled Lemon Garlic Shrimp Skewers

Yield: 4 servings | Prep time: 10 minutes | Cook time: 5 minutes

Ingredients:
- 1 lb large shrimp, peeled and deveined
- 2 cloves garlic, minced
- Zest and juice of 1 lemon
- 2 tablespoons olive oil
- Salt and pepper to taste
- Fresh parsley for garnish

Instructions:
1. In a bowl, combine shrimp, minced garlic, lemon zest, lemon juice, olive oil, salt, and pepper. Toss until shrimp are evenly coated.
2. Thread shrimp onto skewers.
3. Preheat grill to medium-high heat.
4. Grill shrimp skewers for 2-3 minutes per side, or until shrimp are pink and cooked through.
5. Garnish with fresh parsley before serving.

Nutritional information (approximate):
Calories: 160kcal | Protein: 24g | Carbohydrates: 1g | Fat: 7g | Cholesterol: 170mg | Sodium: 160mg

Broiled Cod with Tomato Basil Salsa

Yield: 4 servings | Prep time: 10 minutes | Cook time: 15minutes

Ingredients:
- 4 cod fillets
- 2 tomatoes, diced
- 1/4 cup chopped fresh basil
- 2 tablespoons extra virgin olive oil
- 1 tablespoon balsamic vinegar
- Salt and pepper to taste

Instructions:
1. Preheat broiler to high.
2. Place cod fillets on a baking sheet lined with foil.
3. In a bowl, mix diced tomatoes, chopped basil, olive oil, balsamic vinegar, salt, and pepper to make the salsa.
4. Spoon the salsa over the cod fillets.
5. Broil for 8-10 minutes, or until cod is cooked through and flakes easily with a fork.
6. Serve hot.

Nutritional information (approximate per serving):
Calories: 180kcal | Protein: 22g | Carbohydrates: 3g | Fat: 9g | Cholesterol: 50mg | Sodium: 200mg

Grilled Swordfish with Mango Salsa

Yield: 4 servings | Prep time: 10 minutes | Cook time: 15 minutes

Ingredients:
- 4 swordfish steaks
- 1 ripe mango, diced
- 1/4 cup red bell pepper, diced
- 1/4 cup red onion, finely chopped
- 1 jalapeno, seeded and minced

- 2 tablespoons chopped fresh cilantro
- Juice of 1 lime
- Salt and pepper to taste

Instructions:
1. Preheat grill to medium-high heat.
2. Season swordfish steaks with salt and pepper.
3. Grill swordfish steaks for 4-5 minutes per side, or until cooked through and grill marks appear.
4. In a bowl, combine diced mango, red bell pepper, red onion, jalapeno, cilantro, lime juice, salt, and pepper to make the salsa.
5. Serve grilled swordfish topped with mango salsa.

Nutritional information (approximate):
Calories: 250kcal | Protein: 30g | Carbohydrates: 10g | Fat: 10g | Cholesterol: 70mg | Sodium: 220mg

Pan-Seared Scallops with Garlic Herb Butter

Yield: 4 servings | Prep time: 10 minutes | Cook time: 15 minutes

Ingredients:
- 1 lb. sea scallops
- 2 tablespoons unsalted butter
- 2 cloves garlic, minced
- 1 tablespoon chopped fresh parsley
- Juice of 1 lemon
- Salt and pepper to taste

Instructions:
1. Pat scallops dry with paper towels and season with salt and pepper.
2. Heat butter in a large skillet over medium-high heat. Add minced garlic and cook until fragrant.
3. Add scallops to the skillet and sear for 2-3 minutes per side, or until golden brown and cooked through.
4. Sprinkle chopped parsley over the scallops and squeeze lemon juice on top.
5. Serve hot.
Nutritional information (approximate):
Calories: 200kcal | Protein: 25g | Carbohydrates: 5g | Fat: 9g | Cholesterol: 50mg | Sodium: 570mg

Grilled Mahi Mahi with Pineapple Salsa

Yield: 4 servings | Prep time: 10 minutes | Cook time: 15 minutes

Ingredients:
- 4 Mahi Mahi fillets
- 1 cup diced pineapple
- 1/4 cup red bell pepper, diced
- 1/4 cup red onion, finely chopped
- 1 jalapeno, seeded and minced
- 2 tablespoons chopped fresh cilantro
- Juice of 1 lime
- Salt and pepper to taste

Instructions:
1. Preheat grill to medium-high heat.
2. Season Mahi Mahi fillets with salt and pepper.
3. Grill Mahi Mahi fillets for 4-5 minutes per side, or until cooked through and grill marks appear.
4. In a bowl, combine diced pineapple, red bell pepper, red onion, jalapeno, cilantro, lime juice, salt, and pepper to make the salsa.
5. Serve grilled Mahi Mahi topped with pineapple salsa.

Nutritional information (approximate):
Calories: 220kcal | Protein: 30g | Carbohydrates: 10g | Fat: 6g | Cholesterol: 100mg | Sodium: 180

Grilled Tuna Steaks with Mango Salsa

Yield: 4 servings | Prep time: 15minutes | Cook time: 8 minutes

Ingredients:
- 4 tuna steaks
- 2 ripe mangoes, diced

- 1/2 red bell pepper, diced
- 1/4 cup red onion, finely chopped
- 1/4 cup fresh cilantro, chopped
- Juice of 1 lime
- Salt and pepper to taste

Directions:
1. Preheat grill to medium-high heat.
2. Season tuna steaks with salt and pepper.
3. Grill tuna steaks for about 3-4 minutes per side, or until desired doneness.
4. In a bowl, combine diced mangoes, red bell pepper, red onion, cilantro, lime juice, salt, and pepper to make the salsa.
5. Serve grilled tuna steaks topped with mango salsa.

Nutritional Information (approximate):
Calories: 280kcal | Protein: 35g | Carbohydrates: 20g | Fat: 7g | Cholesterol: 60mg | Sodium: 80mg | Fiber: 4g | Potassium: 850mg

Herb-Baked Tilapia with Lemon Quinoa

Yield: 4 servings | Prep time: 15 minutes | Cook time: 20 minutes

Ingredients:
- 4 tilapia fillets
- 1 tablespoon olive oil
- 1 tablespoon fresh parsley, chopped
- 1 tablespoon fresh dill, chopped
- 1 teaspoon dried oregano
- Salt and pepper to taste
- 1 cup quinoa
- 2 cups water
- Juice and zest of 1 lemon
- 2 tablespoons fresh parsley, chopped

Directions:
1. Preheat the oven to 375°F (190°C).
2. In a small bowl, mix together olive oil, chopped parsley, dill, oregano, salt, and pepper.
3. Place tilapia fillets on a baking sheet lined with parchment paper. Brush the herb mixture over the tilapia fillets.
4. Bake in the preheated oven for 15-20 minutes, or until the fish is cooked through and flakes easily with a fork.
5. While the tilapia is baking, rinse quinoa under cold water. In a saucepan, bring water to a boil. Add quinoa, reduce heat to low, cover, and simmer for 15 minutes, or until quinoa is cooked and water is absorbed.
6. Fluff cooked quinoa with a fork and stir in lemon juice, lemon zest, and chopped parsley. Season with salt and pepper if desired.
7. Serve herb-baked tilapia alongside lemon quinoa.

Nutritional Information (approximate):
Calories: 320kcal | Protein: 30g | Carbohydrates: 25g | Fat: 10g | Cholesterol: 60mg | Sodium: 60mg | Fiber: 4g | Potassium: 600mg

Shrimp Scampi with Whole Wheat Pasta

Yield: 4 servings | Prep time: 10 minutes | Cook time: 15 minutes

Ingredients:
- 8 oz whole wheat pasta
- 1 lb large shrimp, peeled and deveined
- 4 cloves garlic, minced
- 1/4 cup fresh parsley, chopped
- 1/4 cup white wine (optional)
- 2 tablespoons olive oil
- Juice of 1 lemon
- Salt and pepper to taste
- Red pepper flakes (optional)
- Grated Parmesan cheese for serving

Directions:
1. Cook whole wheat pasta according to package instructions until al dente. Drain and set aside.
2. In a large skillet, heat olive oil over medium heat. Add minced garlic and cook until fragrant, about 1 minute.
3. Add shrimp to the skillet and cook until pink and opaque, about 2-3 minutes per side.
4. Pour in white wine (if using) and lemon juice. Add chopped parsley and season with salt,

pepper, and red pepper flakes to taste. Cook for another 2 minutes.
5. Add cooked whole wheat pasta to the skillet and toss until well combined with the shrimp and sauce.
6. Serve hot, garnished with grated Parmesan cheese if desired.

Nutritional Information (approximate):
Calories: 380kcal | Protein: 30g | Carbohydrates: 40g | Fat: 10g | Cholesterol: 200mg | Sodium: 320mg | Fiber: 6g | Potassium: 500mg

Seared Scallops with Sweet Corn Puree

Yield: 4 servings | Prep time: 10 minutes | Cook time: 15 minutes

Ingredients:
- 12 large scallops
- 2 cups sweet corn kernels (fresh or frozen)
- 1/2 cup vegetable or chicken broth
- 2 tablespoons unsalted butter
- 2 cloves garlic, minced
- Salt and pepper to taste
- Fresh parsley or chives for garnish (optional)

Directions:
1. In a blender or food processor, puree the sweet corn kernels with vegetable or chicken broth until smooth. Set aside.
2. Pat dry the scallops with paper towels and season with salt and pepper.
3. Heat a skillet over medium-high heat. Add the butter and minced garlic, then sear the scallops for 2-3 minutes on each side, or until golden brown and cooked through.
4. While the scallops are cooking, reheat the sweet corn puree in a saucepan over medium heat until warmed through.
5. To serve, spoon the sweet corn puree onto plates and top with seared scallops. Garnish with fresh parsley or chives if desired.

Nutritional Information (approximate):
Calories: 280kcal | Protein: 20g | Carbohydrates: 20g | Fat: 12g | Cholesterol: 45mg | Sodium: 400mg | Fiber: 3g | Potassium: 500mg

Grilled Salmon with Dill and Lemon

Yield: 4 servings | Prep time: 10 minutes | Cook time: 10 minutes

Ingredients:
- 4 salmon fillets (about 6 oz each), skin-on
- 2 tablespoons olive oil
- 2 tablespoons fresh dill, chopped
- 2 cloves garlic, minced
- 1 lemon, thinly sliced
- Salt and pepper, to taste

Directions:
1. Preheat the grill to medium-high heat.
2. In a small bowl, mix olive oil, chopped dill, minced garlic, salt, and pepper.
3. Brush both sides of the salmon fillets with the olive oil mixture.
4. Place lemon slices on top of each salmon fillet.
5. Grill the salmon for about 4-5 minutes per side, or until it flakes easily with a fork.
6. Remove the salmon from the grill and serve hot, garnished with additional fresh dill and lemon slices if desired.

Nutritional Information (approximate):
Calories: 350kcal | Protein: 34g | Carbohydrates: 2g | Fat: 23g | Cholesterol: 95mg | Sodium: 70mg | Fiber: 0g | Potassium: 780mg

Lemon Garlic Shrimp Skewers with Asparagus

Yield: 4 servings | Prep time: 15 minutes | Cook time: 8 minutes

Ingredients:
- 1 lb. large shrimp, peeled and deveined
- 1 bunch asparagus, trimmed
- 2 tablespoons olive oil

- 4 cloves garlic, minced
- 1 lemon, zested and juiced
- Salt and pepper, to taste
- Wooden or metal skewers

Directions:
1. If using wooden skewers, soak them in water for 30 minutes to prevent burning.
2. In a small bowl, whisk together olive oil, minced garlic, lemon zest, lemon juice, salt, and pepper to create the marinade.
3. Thread shrimp and asparagus onto skewers, alternating between them.
4. Place the skewers in a shallow dish and pour the marinade over them, ensuring they are evenly coated. Let them marinate for 10-15 minutes.
5. Preheat the grill to medium-high heat. Grill the skewers for about 3-4 minutes per side, or until the shrimp are pink and opaque and the asparagus is tender.
6. Remove from the grill and serve hot.

Nutritional Information (approximate):
Calories: 180kcal | Protein: 24g | Carbohydrates: 6g | Fat: 7g | Cholesterol: 180mg | Sodium: 180mg | Fiber: 3g | Potassium: 400mg

Baked Cod with Tomatoes, Olives, and Capers

Yield: 4 servings | Prep time: 10 minutes | Cook time: 20 minutes

Ingredients:
- 4 cod fillets (about 6 oz each)
- 1 cup cherry tomatoes, halved
- 1/4 cup Kalamata olives, pitted and halved
- 2 tablespoons capers, drained
- 2 cloves garlic, minced
- 2 tablespoons olive oil
- 1 tablespoon fresh parsley, chopped
- Salt and pepper, to taste
- Lemon wedges, for serving

Directions:
1. Preheat the oven to 375°F (190°C).
2. In a baking dish, arrange the cod fillets in a single layer.
3. Scatter halved cherry tomatoes, halved Kalamata olives, drained capers, and minced garlic around the cod fillets.
4. Drizzle olive oil over the cod and tomato mixture. Season everything with salt and pepper.
5. Bake in the preheated oven for 15-20 minutes, or until the cod is opaque and flakes easily with a fork.
6. Remove from the oven and garnish with chopped fresh parsley. Serve hot with lemon wedges on the side.

Nutritional Information (approximate):
Calories: 220kcal | Protein: 26g | Carbohydrates: 5g | Fat: 11g | Cholesterol: 60mg | Sodium: 450mg | Fiber: 2g | Potassium: 580mg

Spicy Grilled Shrimp with Yogurt Sauce

Yield: 4 servings | Prep time: 15 minutes | Cook time: 8 minutes

Ingredients:
- 1 lb (450g) large shrimp, peeled and deveined
- 2 tablespoons olive oil
- 1 teaspoon paprika
- 1/2 teaspoon cayenne pepper
- 1/2 teaspoon garlic powder
- Salt and pepper to taste
- Wooden or metal skewers
- For Yogurt Sauce:
  - 1/2 cup Greek yogurt
  - 1 tablespoon lemon juice
  - 1 tablespoon chopped fresh dill
  - Salt and pepper to taste

Directions:
1. If using wooden skewers, soak them in water for at least 30 minutes to prevent burning.
2. In a small bowl, mix olive oil, paprika, cayenne pepper, garlic powder, salt, and pepper to create a marinade. Add shrimp to the marinade and toss to coat.
3. Thread shrimp onto skewers.

4. Preheat a grill or grill pan over medium-high heat. Grill the shrimp skewers for about 2-3 minutes on each side, or until the shrimp are pink and opaque.
5. In another small bowl, mix together Greek yogurt, lemon juice, chopped fresh dill, salt, and pepper to make the yogurt sauce.
6. Serve the spicy grilled shrimp hot with the yogurt sauce on the side.

Nutritional Information (approximate per serving):
Calories: 200kcal | Protein: 25g | Carbohydrates: 5g | Fat: 9g | Cholesterol: 200mg | Sodium: 300mg | Fiber: 1g | Potassium: 300mg

Tilapia Tacos with Cabbage Slaw

Yield: 4 servings | Prep time: 20 minutes | Cook time: 10 minutes

Ingredients:
- 1 lb (450g) tilapia fillets
- 2 tablespoons olive oil
- 1 teaspoon chili powder
- 1/2 teaspoon cumin
- 1/2 teaspoon garlic powder
- Salt and pepper to taste
- 8 small tortillas (corn or flour)
- For Cabbage Slaw:
  - 2 cups shredded cabbage
  - 1/4 cup chopped cilantro
  - 2 tablespoons lime juice
  - 1 tablespoon olive oil
  - Salt and pepper to taste
- Optional toppings: diced avocado, sliced jalapeños, salsa, sour cream

Directions:
1. In a small bowl, mix olive oil, chili powder, cumin, garlic powder, salt, and pepper to create a marinade. Coat tilapia fillets with the marinade.
2. Preheat a grill or grill pan over medium-high heat. Grill the tilapia fillets for about 3-4 minutes on each side, or until cooked through and flaky.
3. While the tilapia is cooking, prepare the cabbage slaw by mixing shredded cabbage, chopped cilantro, lime juice, olive oil, salt, and pepper in a bowl.
4. Warm tortillas on the grill or in a skillet for about 30 seconds on each side.
5. To assemble the tacos, place a grilled tilapia fillet on each tortilla and top with cabbage slaw and any optional toppings.
6. Serve the tilapia tacos hot and enjoy!

Nutritional Information (approximate per serving):
Calories: 250kcal | Protein: 20g | Carbohydrates: 20g | Fat: 10g | Cholesterol: 40mg | Sodium: 300mg | Fiber: 5g | Potassium: 400mg

Herb-Crusted Halibut

Yield: 4 servings | Prep time: 10 minutes | Cook time: 15 minutes

Ingredients:
- 1 lb (450g) halibut fillets
- 2 tablespoons olive oil
- 1/4 cup breadcrumbs
- 2 tablespoons grated Parmesan cheese
- 1 tablespoon chopped fresh parsley
- 1 teaspoon dried basil
- 1 teaspoon dried thyme
- Salt and pepper to taste
- Lemon wedges for serving

Directions:
1. Preheat the oven to 400°F (200°C).
2. Pat halibut fillets dry with paper towels and place them on a baking sheet lined with parchment paper.
3. In a small bowl, mix olive oil, breadcrumbs, grated Parmesan cheese, chopped fresh parsley, dried basil, dried thyme, salt, and pepper to create the herb crust.
4. Spread the herb crust mixture evenly over the top of each halibut fillet, pressing gently to adhere.
5. Bake in the preheated oven for about 12-15 minutes, or until the halibut is cooked through and the crust is golden brown.

6. Serve the herb-crusted halibut hot, with lemon wedges on the side for squeezing over the fish.

Nutritional Information (approximate per serving):
Calories: 250kcal | Protein: 30g | Carbohydrates: 5g | Fat: 10g | Cholesterol: 60mg | Sodium: 300mg | Fiber: 1g | Potassium: 500mg

Vegetarian Dishes

Quinoa Stuffed Bell Peppers

Yield: 4 servings | Prep Time: 20 minutes | Cook Time: 35 minutes

Ingredients:
- 4 large bell peppers, tops cut off and seeds removed
- 1 cup cooked quinoa
- 1 cup black beans, drained and rinsed
- 1 cup corn kernels (fresh or frozen)
- 1/2 cup diced tomatoes
- 1/2 cup shredded low-fat cheddar cheese
- 1/4 cup finely chopped red onion
- 2 cloves garlic, minced
- 1 tsp ground cumin
- 1 tsp chili powder
- Salt and pepper to taste
- Fresh cilantro for garnish

Directions:
1. Preheat the oven to 375°F. In a large bowl, mix the cooked quinoa, black beans, corn, tomatoes, half of the cheese, onion, garlic, cumin, chili powder, salt, and pepper.
2. Stuff the quinoa mixture into the hollowed bell peppers and place them in a baking dish.
3. Cover with foil and bake for about 30 minutes. Uncover, top with the remaining cheese, and bake for another 5 minutes or until the cheese is melted and bubbly.
4. Garnish with fresh cilantro before serving.

Nutritional Information (approximate per serving):
Calories: 290kcal | Protein: 15g | Carbohydrates: 45g | Fat: 5g | Cholesterol: 10mg | Sodium: 200mg | Fiber: 9g | Potassium: 600mg

Lentil and Vegetable Stew

Yield: 4 servings | Prep Time: 15 minutes | Cook Time: 45 minutes

Ingredients:
- 1 cup dried green lentils, rinsed and drained
- 1 tablespoon olive oil
- 1 large onion, diced
- 2 carrots, peeled and diced
- 2 celery stalks, diced
- 3 garlic cloves, minced
- 1 can (14.5 ounces) diced tomatoes; no salt added
- 4 cups low-sodium vegetable broth
- 2 teaspoons dried thyme
- 2 teaspoons dried oregano
- Salt and black pepper to taste
- 2 cups chopped kale or spinach
- 1 tablespoon lemon juice (optional)

Directions:
1. Heat olive oil in a large pot over medium heat. Add onion, carrots, and celery, and sauté until softened.
2. Stir in garlic and cook for another minute until fragrant.
3. Add lentils, diced tomatoes, vegetable broth, thyme, oregano, salt, and pepper.
4. Bring to a boil, then reduce heat and simmer for about 30 minutes, until lentils are tender.
5. Add kale or spinach and cook until the greens have wilted. Stir in lemon juice if using, adjust seasoning, and serve warm.

Nutritional Information (approximate per serving):
Calories: 250kcal | Protein: 18g | Carbohydrates: 38g | Fat: 4g | Cholesterol: 0mg | Sodium: 300mg | Fiber: 15g | Potassium: 710mg

Garlic Roasted Cauliflower Steaks

Yield: 4 servings | Prep Time: 10 minutes | Cook Time: 25 minutes

Ingredients:
- 1 large head of cauliflower
- 4 tablespoons olive oil
- 4 garlic cloves, minced
- Salt and pepper to taste
- Fresh parsley, chopped (for garnish)

Directions:
1. Preheat the oven to 400°F. Slice the cauliflower head into 1/2-inch-thick steaks.
2. Arrange the cauliflower steaks on a baking sheet. Drizzle with olive oil and sprinkle with minced garlic, salt, and pepper.
3. Roast in the oven for 20-25 minutes or until the cauliflower is golden and tender.
4. Garnish with fresh parsley before serving.

Nutritional Information (approximate per serving):
Calories: 150kcal | Protein: 3g | Carbohydrates: 10g | Fat: 11g | Cholesterol: 0mg | Sodium: 30mg | Fiber: 4g | Potassium: 450mg

Tofu and Broccoli Stir-Fry

Yield: 4 servings | Prep Time: 15 minutes | Cook Time: 10 minutes

Ingredients:
- 1 block (14 ounces) firm tofu, drained and cut into cubes
- 4 cups broccoli florets
- 2 tablespoons soy sauce (low sodium)
- 1 tablespoon sesame oil
- 2 cloves garlic, minced
- 1 tablespoon fresh ginger, minced
- 1 tablespoon olive oil
- Optional: sesame seeds for garnish

Directions:
1. Press the tofu to remove excess moisture and then cut into cubes.
2. Heat olive oil in a large skillet or wok over medium-high heat. Add tofu and cook until golden brown on all sides.
3. Add the garlic and ginger to the pan, stir-frying quickly to prevent burning.
4. Add the broccoli and stir-fry until it is bright green and tender-crisp.
5. Drizzle with soy sauce and sesame oil, mixing well to coat the tofu and broccoli.
6. Serve hot, garnished with sesame seeds if desired.

Nutritional Information (approximate per serving):
Calories: 150kcal | Protein: 12g | Carbohydrates: 10g | Fat: 8g | Cholesterol: 0mg | Sodium: 300mg | Fiber: 3g | Potassium: 300mg

Spaghetti Squash with Marinara Sauce

Yield: 4 servings | Prep time: 10 minutes | Cook time: 40 minutes

Ingredients:
- 1 medium spaghetti squash
- 2 cups marinara sauce

- 1 tablespoon olive oil
- Salt and pepper to taste
- Optional: grated Parmesan cheese and fresh basil for garnish

Directions:
1. Preheat the oven to 400°F (200°C).
2. Cut the spaghetti squash in half lengthwise and scoop out the seeds.
3. Rub the cut sides of the squash with olive oil and season with salt and pepper.
4. Place the squash halves cut side down on a baking sheet and bake for 30-40 minutes, or until tender when pierced with a fork.
5. While the squash is baking, heat the marinara sauce in a saucepan over medium heat until warmed through.
6. Once the squash is done, use a fork to scrape the flesh into spaghetti-like strands.
7. Serve the spaghetti squash topped with marinara sauce. Optionally, garnish with grated Parmesan cheese and fresh basil.

Nutritional information (approximate per serving):
Calories: 160kcal | Protein: 3g | Carbohydrates: 28g | Fat: 5g | Cholesterol: 0mg | Sodium: 700mg | Fiber: 6g | Potassium: 560mg

Black Bean and Corn Tacos

Yield: 4 servings | Prep time: 10 minutes | Cook time: 15 minutes

Ingredients:
- 8 small corn tortillas
- 1 can (15 oz) black beans, drained and rinsed
- 1 cup frozen corn, thawed
- 1 small red onion, diced
- 1 teaspoon ground cumin
- 1 teaspoon chili powder
- Salt and pepper to taste
- Optional toppings: shredded lettuce, diced tomatoes, avocado slices, salsa, lime wedges

Directions:
1. In a skillet over medium heat, warm the corn tortillas for about 30 seconds on each side. Keep warm wrapped in a kitchen towel.
2. In the same skillet, add the black beans, corn, and diced red onion. Cook for 5-7 minutes, stirring occasionally.
3. Stir in the ground cumin, chili powder, salt, and pepper. Cook for an additional 2-3 minutes until the mixture is heated through and flavors are well combined.
4. To assemble the tacos, spoon the black bean and corn mixture onto each warm tortilla. Top with desired toppings such as shredded lettuce, diced tomatoes, avocado slices, salsa, and a squeeze of lime juice.

Nutritional information (approximate per serving):
Calories: 260kcal | Protein: 9g | Carbohydrates: 51g | Fat: 2g | Cholesterol: 0mg | Sodium: 430mg | Fiber: 10g | Potassium: 610mg

Vegetarian Chili with Quinoa

Yield: 4 servings | Prep time: 15 minutes | Cook time: 30 minutes

Ingredients:
- 1 tablespoon olive oil
- 1 small onion, diced
- 2 cloves garlic, minced
- 1 bell pepper, diced
- 1 zucchini, diced
- 1 can (15 oz) diced tomatoes
- 1 can (15 oz) black beans, drained and rinsed
- 1 cup cooked quinoa
- 2 cups vegetable broth
- 1 tablespoon chili powder
- 1 teaspoon ground cumin
- Salt and pepper to taste
- Optional toppings: chopped cilantro, diced avocado, shredded cheese, sour cream

Directions:
1. In a large pot, heat the olive oil over medium heat. Add the diced onion and minced garlic, and cook until softened, about 3-4 minutes.
2. Add the diced bell pepper and zucchini to the pot and cook for another 3-4 minutes until they begin to soften.
3. Stir in the diced tomatoes, black beans, cooked quinoa, vegetable broth, chili powder,

ground cumin, salt, and pepper. Bring the mixture to a simmer.
4. Reduce the heat to low, cover the pot, and let the chili simmer for 20-25 minutes, stirring occasionally.
5. Once the chili has thickened and the vegetables are tender, adjust seasoning if needed. Serve hot, garnished with optional toppings if desired.

Nutritional information (approximate per serving):
Calories: 290kcal | Protein: 11g | Carbohydrates: 49g | Fat: 6g | Cholesterol: 0mg | Sodium: 830mg | Fiber: 12g | Potassium: 820mg

Zucchini Noodles with Pesto

Yield: 4 servings | Prep time: 15 minutes | Cook time: 10 minutes

Ingredients:
- 4 medium zucchinis
- 1 cup fresh basil leaves
- 1/4 cup pine nuts
- 2 cloves garlic
- 1/4 cup grated Parmesan cheese
- 1/4 cup olive oil
- Salt and pepper to taste
- Optional: cherry tomatoes, additional Parmesan cheese for garnish

Directions:
1. Using a spiralizer or vegetable peeler, create zucchini noodles (zoodles) from the zucchinis. Set aside.
2. In a food processor, combine the fresh basil leaves, pine nuts, garlic, and grated Parmesan cheese. Pulse until finely chopped.
3. With the food processor running, slowly drizzle in the olive oil until the pesto is smooth and well combined. Season with salt and pepper to taste.
4. Heat a large skillet over medium heat. Add the zucchini noodles and cook for 3-5 minutes, tossing occasionally, until they are just tender.
5. Remove the skillet from heat and stir in the pesto until the zucchini noodles are evenly coated. Serve immediately, garnished with cherry tomatoes and additional Parmesan cheese if desired.

Nutritional information (approximate per serving):
Calories: 220kcal | Protein: 6g | Carbohydrates: 8g | Fat: 20g | Cholesterol: 5mg | Sodium: 160mg | Fiber: 3g | Potassium: 600mg

Baked Cod with Olive Tapenade

Yield: 4 servings | Prep time: 10 minutes | Cook time: 20 minutes

Ingredients:
- 4 cod fillets (about 6 oz each)
- 1 cup pitted Kalamata olives
- 2 cloves garlic
- 2 tablespoons capers
- 2 tablespoons fresh parsley
- 2 tablespoons lemon juice
- 2 tablespoons olive oil
- Salt and pepper to taste

Directions:
1. Preheat the oven to 400°F (200°C). Place the cod fillets in a baking dish and season with salt and pepper.
2. In a food processor, combine the Kalamata olives, garlic, capers, parsley, lemon juice, and olive oil. Pulse until the mixture forms a coarse paste.
3. Spoon the olive tapenade evenly over the top of each cod fillet, pressing gently to adhere.
4. Bake the cod in the preheated oven for 15-20 minutes, or until the fish is cooked through and flakes easily with a fork.
5. Serve the baked cod hot, garnished with additional fresh parsley and lemon wedges if desired.

Nutritional information (approximate per serving):
Calories: 280kcal | Protein: 25g | Carbohydrates: 4g | Fat: 18g | Cholesterol: 50mg | Sodium: 800mg | Fiber: 2g | Potassium: 630mg

Stuffed Eggplant with Lentils

Yield: 4 servings | Prep time: 15 minutes | Cook time: 40 minutes

Ingredients:
- 2 large eggplants
- 1 cup dry lentils
- 2 cups vegetable broth
- 1 small onion, diced
- 2 cloves garlic, minced
- 1 bell pepper, diced
- 1 teaspoon dried oregano
- 1 teaspoon dried basil
- Salt and pepper to taste
- 1/4 cup grated Parmesan cheese (optional)

Directions:
1. Preheat the oven to 375°F (190°C). Cut the eggplants in half lengthwise and scoop out the flesh, leaving about 1/4-inch-thick shells. Chop the scooped-out flesh and set aside.
2. Rinse the lentils under cold water and drain. In a saucepan, combine the lentils and vegetable broth. Bring to a boil, then reduce heat to low and simmer for 20-25 minutes, or until the lentils are tender.
3. In a separate skillet, heat some olive oil over medium heat. Add the diced onion, minced garlic, and diced bell pepper. Cook until softened, about 5 minutes.
4. Add the chopped eggplant flesh to the skillet along with the dried oregano, dried basil, salt, and pepper. Cook for another 5 minutes, until the eggplant is tender.
5. Stir the cooked lentils into the skillet with the vegetable mixture. Spoon the mixture into the eggplant shells and place them in a baking dish. If desired, sprinkle grated Parmesan cheese on top.
6. Bake in the preheated oven for 15-20 minutes, or until the eggplant is tender and the filling is heated through.

Nutritional information (approximate):
Calories: 290kcal | Protein: 17g | Carbohydrates: 52g | Fat: 2g | Cholesterol: 0mg | Sodium: 460mg | Fiber: 19g | Potassium: 1300mg

Lentil and Walnut Burgers

Yield: 4 servings | Prep time: 15 minutes | Cook time: 20 minutes

Ingredients:
- 1 cup cooked lentils
- 1 cup walnuts, finely chopped
- 1/2 cup breadcrumbs
- 1/4 cup finely chopped onion
- 2 cloves garlic, minced
- 1 tablespoon soy sauce
- 1 teaspoon smoked paprika
- Salt and pepper, to taste
- 1 tablespoon olive oil (for cooking)

Directions:
1. In a large mixing bowl, combine cooked lentils, chopped walnuts, breadcrumbs, onion, garlic, soy sauce, smoked paprika, salt, and pepper. Mix well until all ingredients are evenly distributed.
2. Form the mixture into burger patties, using about 1/2 cup of the mixture for each patty.
3. Heat olive oil in a skillet over medium heat. Cook the burger patties for about 4-5 minutes on each side, or until they are golden brown and heated through.
4. Serve the lentil and walnut burgers on buns with your favorite toppings and condiments.

Nutritional information (approximate per serving):
Calories: 342kcal | Protein: 14g | Carbohydrates: 30g | Fat: 20g | Cholesterol: 0mg | Sodium: 317mg | Fiber: 9g | Potassium: 428mg

Tofu Stir-Fry with Vegetables

Yield: 4 servings | Prep time: 15 minutes | Cook time: 15 minutes

Ingredients:
- 14 ounces extra-firm tofu, pressed and cubed

- 2 tablespoons soy sauce
- 2 tablespoons hoisin sauce
- 1 tablespoon rice vinegar
- 1 tablespoon sesame oil
- 2 tablespoons vegetable oil
- 2 cloves garlic, minced
- 1 teaspoon grated ginger
- 1 bell pepper, sliced
- 1 cup broccoli florets
- 1 cup sliced carrots
- 1 cup snow peas
- Cooked rice or noodles, for serving

Directions:
1. In a small bowl, mix the soy sauce, hoisin sauce, rice vinegar, and sesame oil to make the sauce. Set aside.
2. Heat 1 tablespoon of vegetable oil in a large skillet or wok over medium-high heat. Add the cubed tofu and cook until golden brown on all sides, about 5-7 minutes. Remove the tofu from the skillet and set aside.
3. In the same skillet, add the remaining tablespoon of vegetable oil. Add the minced garlic and grated ginger, and sauté for about 30 seconds until fragrant.
4. Add the sliced bell pepper, broccoli florets, sliced carrots, and snow peas to the skillet. Stir-fry for about 5-7 minutes, or until the vegetables are tender-crisp.
5. Return the cooked tofu to the skillet and pour the sauce over the tofu and vegetables. Stir well to coat everything evenly with the sauce.
6. Serve the tofu stir-fry with vegetables over cooked rice or noodles.

Nutritional information (approximate per serving):
Calories: 278kcal | Protein: 14g | Carbohydrates: 16g | Fat: 18g | Cholesterol: 0mg | Sodium: 686mg | Fiber: 4g | Potassium: 491mg

Seitan Beef Stew

Yield: 4 servings | Prep time: 20 minutes | Cook time: 40 minutes

Ingredients:
- 1 tablespoon olive oil
- 1 onion, diced
- 2 cloves garlic, minced
- 2 carrots, sliced
- 2 celery stalks, sliced
- 1 cup diced potatoes
- 1 cup diced tomatoes
- 4 cups vegetable broth
- 1 cup seitan beef, cubed
- 1 teaspoon dried thyme
- 1 teaspoon dried rosemary
- Salt and pepper, to taste
- Chopped fresh parsley, for garnish (optional)

Directions:
1. In a large pot, heat the olive oil over medium heat. Add the diced onion and minced garlic, and sauté until softened, about 3-4 minutes.
2. Add the sliced carrots, celery, and diced potatoes to the pot. Stir well and cook for another 5 minutes.
3. Pour in the diced tomatoes and vegetable broth. Bring the mixture to a boil, then reduce the heat to low and let it simmer for 15 minutes, or until the vegetables are tender.
4. Add the cubed seitan beef, dried thyme, dried rosemary, salt, and pepper to the pot. Stir well and let the stew simmer for another 10 minutes to allow the flavors to meld together.
5. Taste and adjust seasoning if needed. Serve the seitan beef stew hot, garnished with chopped fresh parsley if desired.

Nutritional information (approximate per serving):
Calories: 229kcal | Protein: 15g | Carbohydrates: 27g | Fat: 7g | Cholesterol: 0mg | Sodium: 981mg | Fiber: 5g | Potassium: 594mg

Black Bean and Sweet Potato Chili

Yield: 4 servings | Prep time: 15 minutes | Cook time: 30 minutes

Ingredients:
- 1 tablespoon olive oil
- 1 onion, diced
- 2 cloves garlic, minced
- 2 sweet potatoes, peeled and diced
- 1 bell pepper, diced

- 1 can (15 ounces) black beans, drained and rinsed
- 1 can (14.5 ounces) diced tomatoes
- 2 cups vegetable broth
- 2 teaspoons chili powder
- 1 teaspoon ground cumin
- 1/2 teaspoon smoked paprika
- Salt and pepper, to taste
- Optional toppings: diced avocado, chopped cilantro, shredded cheese, sour cream

Directions:
1. Heat olive oil in a large pot over medium heat. Add diced onion and minced garlic, and sauté until softened, about 3-4 minutes.
2. Add diced sweet potatoes and bell pepper to the pot. Cook for another 5 minutes, stirring occasionally.
3. Stir in black beans, diced tomatoes (with their juices), vegetable broth, chili powder, ground cumin, smoked paprika, salt, and pepper.
4. Bring the chili to a boil, then reduce the heat to low and let it simmer for about 20 minutes, or until the sweet potatoes are tender.
5. Taste and adjust seasoning if necessary. Serve the black bean and sweet potato chili hot, garnished with optional toppings if desired.

Nutritional information (approximate):
Calories: 297kcal | Protein: 9g | Carbohydrates: 52g | Fat: 7g | Cholesterol: 0mg | Sodium: 769mg | Fiber: 11g | Potassium: 918mg

Tempeh Bacon BLT

Yield: 4 servings | Prep time: 10 minutes | Cook time: 10 minutes

Ingredients:
- 8 ounces tempeh, sliced thinly
- 2 tablespoons soy sauce
- 1 tablespoon maple syrup
- 1 tablespoon apple cider vinegar
- 1 teaspoon liquid smoke
- 1/2 teaspoon garlic powder
- 1/2 teaspoon smoked paprika
- 1 tablespoon vegetable oil
- 8 slices bread
- Lettuce leaves
- Tomato slices
- Vegan mayonnaise

Directions:
1. In a shallow dish, whisk together soy sauce, maple syrup, apple cider vinegar, liquid smoke, garlic powder, and smoked paprika to make the marinade.
2. Place tempeh slices in the marinade, ensuring they are well coated. Let them marinate for at least 10 minutes.
3. Heat vegetable oil in a skillet over medium heat. Add the marinated tempeh slices and cook for 3-4 minutes on each side, or until crispy and browned.
4. Toast the bread slices and spread vegan mayonnaise on one side of each slice.
5. Assemble the sandwiches by layering lettuce, tomato slices, and tempeh bacon on the mayo-coated side of 4 bread slices. Top with the remaining bread slices.

Nutritional information (approximate):
Calories: 342kcal | Protein: 20g | Carbohydrates: 40g | Fat: 12g | Cholesterol: 0mg | Sodium: 956mg | Fiber: 6g | Potassium: 498mg

Edamame Hummus Wrap

Yield: 4 servings | Prep time: 15 minutes | Cook time: 0 minutes

Ingredients:
- 1 cup shelled edamame
- 1/4 cup tahini
- 2 tablespoons lemon juice
- 2 cloves garlic, minced
- 1/4 teaspoon ground cumin
- Salt and pepper, to taste
- 4 large tortillas
- 2 cups mixed salad greens
- 1 bell pepper, thinly sliced
- 1 cucumber, thinly sliced
- 1/4 cup sliced red onion

Directions:
1. In a food processor, combine shelled edamame, tahini, lemon juice, minced garlic, ground cumin, salt, and pepper. Blend until

smooth, adding a splash of water if needed to reach desired consistency.
2. Lay out the tortillas on a flat surface. Spread a generous amount of the edamame hummus onto each tortilla.
3. Divide the mixed salad greens, sliced bell pepper, cucumber, and red onion evenly among the tortillas, placing the ingredients in a line down the center of each tortilla.
4. Fold the sides of each tortilla over the filling, then roll tightly to form a wrap.
5. Slice each wrap in half diagonally and serve.

Nutritional information (approximate):
Calories: 302kcal | Protein: 12g | Carbohydrates: 30g | Fat: 16g | Cholesterol: 0mg | Sodium: 229mg | Fiber: 6g | Potassium: 534mg

Vegan Meatloaf with Lentils and Mushrooms

Yield: 4 servings | Prep time: 20 minutes | Cook time: 45 minutes

Ingredients:
- 1 cup cooked lentils
- 1 cup chopped mushrooms
- 1 small onion, finely chopped
- 2 cloves garlic, minced
- 1 tablespoon olive oil
- 1 tablespoon soy sauce
- 1 tablespoon tomato paste
- 1 tablespoon ground flaxseed
- 3/4 cup breadcrumbs
- 1/4 cup chopped fresh parsley
- 1 teaspoon dried thyme
- Salt and pepper, to taste
- Ketchup or BBQ sauce, for topping (optional)

Directions:
1. Preheat the oven to 375°F (190°C). Grease a loaf pan and set aside.
2. In a skillet, heat olive oil over medium heat. Add chopped mushrooms, onion, and minced garlic. Sauté until the vegetables are softened, about 5-7 minutes.
3. In a large mixing bowl, combine cooked lentils, sautéed mushrooms and onion, soy sauce, tomato paste, ground flaxseed, breadcrumbs, chopped parsley, dried thyme, salt, and pepper. Mix until well combined.
4. Transfer the mixture into the greased loaf pan, pressing it down firmly.
5. Bake in the preheated oven for 40-45 minutes, or until the top is golden brown and the edges are crispy.
6. Allow the vegan meatloaf to cool for a few minutes before slicing and serving. Optionally, top with ketchup or BBQ sauce.

Nutritional information (approximate):
Calories: 259kcal | Protein: 12g | Carbohydrates: 38g | Fat: 7g | Cholesterol: 0mg | Sodium: 436mg | Fiber: 9g | Potassium: 511mg

Soy Curl Fajitas

Yield: 4 servings | Prep time: 15 minutes | Cook time: 15 minutes

Ingredients:
- 2 cups dried soy curls
- 2 tablespoons olive oil
- 1 onion, thinly sliced
- 1 bell pepper, thinly sliced
- 1 teaspoon chili powder
- 1 teaspoon ground cumin
- 1/2 teaspoon smoked paprika
- 1/2 teaspoon garlic powder
- Salt and pepper, to taste
- 8 small flour tortillas
- Optional toppings: sliced avocado, salsa, vegan sour cream, shredded lettuce, lime wedges

Directions:
1. Rehydrate the dried soy curls according to package instructions. Drain and set aside.
2. Heat olive oil in a large skillet over medium heat. Add the sliced onion and bell pepper, and sauté until softened, about 5 minutes.
3. Add the rehydrated soy curls to the skillet, along with chili powder, ground cumin, smoked paprika, garlic powder, salt, and pepper. Stir well to coat the soy curls and vegetables with the spices.

4. Cook for another 5-7 minutes, stirring occasionally, until the soy curls are heated through and slightly crispy around the edges.
5. Warm the flour tortillas in a separate skillet or in the microwave. Serve the soy curl mixture in warm tortillas, topped with optional toppings as desired.

Nutritional information (approximate):
Calories: 310kcal | Protein: 18g | Carbohydrates: 35g | Fat: 12g | Cholesterol: 0mg | Sodium: 420mg | Fiber: 8g | Potassium: 540mg

Pea Protein Burgers

Yield: 4 servings | Prep time: 15 minutes | Cook time: 20 minutes

Ingredients:
- 1 cup cooked green peas
- 1 cup cooked quinoa
- 1/2 cup rolled oats
- 1/4 cup pea protein powder
- 1/4 cup chopped onion
- 2 cloves garlic, minced
- 1 tablespoon soy sauce
- 1 teaspoon ground cumin
- Salt and pepper, to taste
- 2 tablespoons olive oil (for cooking)

Directions:
1. In a food processor, combine cooked green peas, cooked quinoa, rolled oats, pea protein powder, chopped onion, minced garlic, soy sauce, ground cumin, salt, and pepper. Pulse until well combined and the mixture holds together.
2. Form the mixture into burger patties, using about 1/2 cup of the mixture for each patty.
3. Heat olive oil in a skillet over medium heat. Cook the burger patties for about 4-5 minutes on each side, or until they are golden brown and heated through.
4. Serve the pea protein burgers on buns with your favorite toppings and condiments.

Nutritional information (approximate per serving):
Calories: 289kcal | Protein: 17g | Carbohydrates: 38g | Fat: 8g | Cholesterol: 0mg | Sodium: 320mg | Fiber: 8g | Potassium: 472mg

Desserts

Fruit Salad with Yogurt

Yield: 4 servings | Prep time: 15 minutes | Cook time: 0 minutes

Ingredients:
- 2 medium bananas, sliced
- 1 apple, cored and chopped
- 1/2 cup of blueberries
- 1/2 cup of strawberries, hulled and halved
- 1/2 cup of grapes, halved
- 1/2 cup of low-fat Greek yogurt
- 1 tablespoon of honey
- 1/2 teaspoon of ground cinnamon

Directions
1. In a large bowl, combine the sliced bananas, chopped apple, blueberries, strawberries, and grapes.
2. In a separate small bowl, mix the Greek yogurt, honey, and cinnamon until well blended.
3. Pour the yogurt mixture over the fruit and gently toss to combine.
4. Serve immediately or chill in the refrigerator for 1 hour before serving for flavors to meld.

Nutritional information (approximate per serving):
Calories: 150kcal | Protein: 4g | Carbohydrates: 34g | Fat: 1g | Cholesterol: 2mg | Sodium: 20mg | Fibber: 4g | Potassium: 450mg

Carrot and Apple Loaf

Yield: 6 servings | Prep time: 15 minutes | Cook time: 45 minutes

Ingredients:
- 1 cup all-purpose flour
- 1/2 cup whole wheat flour
- 1 teaspoon baking powder
- 1/2 teaspoon baking soda
- 1/4 teaspoon salt
- 1 teaspoon ground cinnamon
- 1/2 teaspoon ground nutmeg
- 1/2 cup unsalted butter, melted
- 1/2 cup brown sugar, packed
- 2 large eggs
- 1 teaspoon vanilla extract
- 1 cup grated carrots
- 1 cup grated apples (such as Granny Smith)

Directions:
1. Preheat the oven to 350°F (175°C). Grease and flour a 9x5-inch loaf pan.
2. In a large bowl, whisk together the all-purpose flour, whole wheat flour, baking powder, baking soda, salt, cinnamon, and nutmeg.
3. In another bowl, beat together the melted butter and brown sugar until well combined. Add the eggs, one at a time, beating well after each addition. Stir in the vanilla extract.
4. Gradually add the dry ingredients to the wet ingredients, stirring until just combined. Fold in the grated carrots and apples until evenly distributed.
5. Pour the batter into the prepared loaf pan and smooth the top. Bake for 40-45 minutes, or until a toothpick inserted into the center comes out clean. Allow the loaf to cool in the pan for 10 minutes before transferring to a wire rack to cool completely.

Nutritional information (approximate per serving):
Calories 260kcal | Protein 4g | Carbohydrates 34g | Fat 12g | Cholesterol 75mg | Sodium 210mg | Fiber 2g | Potassium 210mg.

Pear Crumble with Oat Topping

Yield: 4 servings | Prep time: 15 minutes | Cook time: 35 minutes

Ingredients:
- 4 ripe pears, peeled, cored, and sliced
- 2 tablespoons granulated sugar
- 1 tablespoon all-purpose flour
- 1/2 teaspoon ground cinnamon
- 1/4 teaspoon ground nutmeg

For the oat topping:
- 1/2 cup old-fashioned oats
- 1/4 cup all-purpose flour
- 1/4 cup brown sugar, packed
- 1/4 cup unsalted butter, melted
- 1/4 teaspoon salt

Directions:
1. Preheat the oven to 375°F (190°C). Grease a 9-inch pie dish or baking dish.
2. In a large bowl, toss the sliced pears with granulated sugar, flour, cinnamon, and nutmeg until well coated. Transfer the pear mixture to the prepared dish, spreading it out evenly.
3. In another bowl, combine the oats, flour, brown sugar, melted butter, and salt. Mix until the ingredients are evenly distributed, and the mixture is crumbly.
4. Sprinkle the oat topping over the pears in an even layer.
5. Bake for 30-35 minutes, or until the topping is golden brown and the pears are tender when pierced with a fork.
6. Allow the crumble to cool slightly before serving. Serve warm or at room temperature.

Nutritional information (approximate per serving):
Calories 290kcal | Protein 3g | Carbohydrates 49g | Fat 11g | Cholesterol 30mg | Sodium 75mg | Fiber 6g | Potassium 280mg

Red Currant Jelly

Yield: Approximately 3 cups | Prep time: 10 minutes | Cook time: 20 minutes

Ingredients:
- 4 cups red currants
- 1 cup water
- 2 cups granulated sugar

Directions:
1. Rinse the red currants and remove any stems.
2. In a large saucepan, combine the red currants and water. Bring to a boil over medium heat, then reduce the heat to low and simmer for 10 minutes, stirring occasionally.
3. Remove the saucepan from the heat and let the mixture cool slightly. Pour the mixture into a fine mesh sieve or cheesecloth-lined strainer set over a large bowl. Press the currants to extract as much juice as possible.
4. Discard the pulp and return the strained juice to the saucepan. Add the sugar to the juice and stir until dissolved.
5. Bring the mixture to a boil over medium-high heat, then reduce the heat to low and simmer for about 10 minutes, or until the mixture reaches the desired consistency and coats the back of a spoon.
6. Remove the saucepan from the heat and skim off any foam from the surface of the jelly. Pour the hot jelly into clean, sterilized jars and seal with lids. Allow the jelly to cool completely before refrigerating.

Nutritional information (approximate per serving):
Calories 60kcal | Protein 0g | Carbohydrates 15g | Fat 0g | Cholesterol 0mg | Sodium 0mg | Fiber 0g | Potassium 30mg

Cottage Cheese Pudding with Vanilla

Yield: 4 servings | Prep time: 10 minutes | Cook time: 30 minutes

Ingredients:
- 2 cups cottage cheese
- 1/2 cup granulated sugar
- 2 large eggs
- 2 tablespoons all-purpose flour
- 1 teaspoon vanilla extract

Directions:
1. Preheat the oven to 350°F (175°C). Grease a baking dish.
2. In a blender or food processor, blend the cottage cheese until smooth.
3. In a large bowl, whisk together the blended cottage cheese, sugar, eggs, flour, and vanilla extract until well combined.
4. Pour the mixture into the prepared baking dish.
5. Bake for 25-30 minutes, or until the pudding is set and the top is golden brown.
6. Remove from the oven and let cool slightly before serving.

Nutritional information (approximate per serving):
Calories 220kcal | Protein 16g | Carbohydrates 18g | Fat 8g | Cholesterol 110mg | Sodium 420mg | Fiber 0g | Potassium 200mg

Buckwheat Pancakes with Berry Sause

Yield: 4 servings | Prep time: 10 minutes | Cook time: 15 minutes

Ingredients:
For the pancakes:
- 1 cup buckwheat flour
- 1 tablespoon baking powder
- 1/4 teaspoon salt
- 1 tablespoon honey
- 1 cup milk
- 2 large eggs

- 2 tablespoons unsalted butter, melted
- Butter or oil for cooking

For the berry sauce:
- 2 cups mixed berries (such as strawberries, blueberries, raspberries)
- 2 tablespoons honey
- 1 tablespoon lemon juice
- 1/4 cup water

Directions:
1. In a large bowl, whisk together the buckwheat flour, baking powder, and salt.
2. In another bowl, whisk together the honey, milk, eggs, and melted butter until well combined.
3. Pour the wet ingredients into the dry ingredients and stir until just combined. Do not overmix; some lumps are okay.
4. Heat a non-stick skillet or griddle over medium heat and lightly grease with butter or oil.
5. Pour about 1/4 cup of batter onto the skillet for each pancake. Cook until bubbles form on the surface, then flip and cook until golden brown on the other side.
6. Meanwhile, prepare the berry sauce. In a small saucepan, combine the mixed berries, honey, lemon juice, and water. Bring to a simmer over medium heat and cook for 5-7 minutes, or until the berries are soft and the sauce has thickened slightly.
7. Serve the pancakes warm topped with the berry sauce.

Nutritional information (approximate per serving):
Calories 290kcal | Protein 9g | Carbohydrates 42g | Fat 10g | Cholesterol 105mg | Sodium 420mg | Fiber 6g | Potassium 380mg

Strawberry Tiramisu Without Sugar

Yield: 4 servings | Prep time: 20 minutes | Cook time: 0 minutes

Ingredients:
- 8 ounces mascarpone cheese
- 1 cup heavy cream
- 1 teaspoon vanilla extract
- 1 cup fresh strawberries, sliced
- 1/4 cup unsweetened cocoa powder
- 1/4 cup brewed coffee, cooled

Directions:
1. In a mixing bowl, beat the mascarpone cheese until smooth and creamy.
2. In another bowl, whip the heavy cream with vanilla extract until stiff peaks form.
3. Gently fold the whipped cream into the mascarpone cheese until well combined.
4. In a shallow dish, mix the brewed coffee with cocoa powder until smooth.
5. Dip ladyfinger cookies into the coffee mixture and arrange a layer of dipped cookies in the bottom of serving glasses or a baking dish.
6. Top the ladyfingers with a layer of the mascarpone mixture, followed by a layer of sliced strawberries. Repeat the layers until all ingredients are used, ending with a layer of mascarpone mixture on top.
7. Refrigerate the tiramisu for at least 4 hours, or overnight, to allow the flavors to meld and the dessert to set.

Nutritional information (approximate per serving):
Calories 330kcal | Protein 5g | Carbohydrates 8g | Fat 30g | Cholesterol 90mg | Sodium 40mg | Fiber 2g | Potassium 200mg

Cinnamon Apple Chips

Yield: 4 servings | Prep time: 10 minutes | Cook time: 2 hours

Ingredients:
- 4 medium-sized apples, any sweet variety
- 2 teaspoons of ground cinnamon
- 1 tablespoon of granulated sugar (optional)

Directions:
1. Preheat your oven to 200°F (93°C).
2. Core the apples and thinly slice them into rounds.
3. Arrange the apple slices in a single layer on a baking sheet lined with parchment paper.
4. Mix the cinnamon and sugar together and sprinkle over the apple slices.

5. Bake in the preheated oven for 1 hour, then flip the apple slices and continue baking for another 1 hour, or until the apple chips are crispy.
6. Remove from the oven and let them cool completely; they will continue to crisp up as they cool.

Nutritional information (approximate per serving):
Calories: 95kcal | Protein: 0.5g | Carbohydrates: 25g | Fat: 0.3g | Cholesterol: 0mg | Sodium: 2mg | Fiber: 4.4g | Potassium: 195mg

Banana Ice Cream

Yield: 4 servings | Prep time: 5 minutes | Cook time: 0 minutes (Freeze time: 2 hours)

Ingredients:
- 4 large ripe bananas

Directions:
1. Peel the bananas and slice them into 1/2-inch discs.
2. Arrange banana slices in a single layer on a baking sheet, and freeze until solid, about 2 hours.
3. Place frozen banana slices in a food processor or powerful blender and blend until smooth and creamy.
4. For a soft-serve texture, serve immediately. For firmer ice cream, transfer to a container and freeze for an additional hour.

Nutritional information (approximate per serving):
Calories: 105kcal | Protein: 1.3g | Carbohydrates: 27g | Fat: 0.4g | Cholesterol: 0mg | Sodium: 1mg | Fiber: 3.1g | Potassium: 422mg

Avocado Chocolate Pudding

Yield: 4 servings | Prep time: 15 minutes | Cook time: 0 minutes

Ingredients:
- 2 ripe avocados, peeled and pitted
- 1/4 cup unsweetened cocoa powder
- 1/4 cup honey or maple syrup
- 1/4 cup milk (almond milk for vegan option)
- 1 teaspoon pure vanilla extract
- Pinch of salt

Directions:
1. Place the avocados, cocoa powder, honey or maple syrup, milk, vanilla extract, and a pinch of salt in a blender or food processor.
2. Blend on high until smooth and creamy, scraping down the sides as necessary.
3. Taste and adjust sweetness if necessary.
4. Divide the pudding into serving dishes and refrigerate for at least 30 minutes before serving.
5. Garnish with a sprinkle of cocoa powder or shaved dark chocolate before serving if desired.

Nutritional information (approximate per serving):
Calories: 240kcal | Protein: 3g | Carbohydrates: 27g | Fat: 15g | Cholesterol: 0mg | Sodium: 35mg | Fiber: 7g | Potassium: 487mg

Apple Cinnamon Oat Cookies

Yield: 6 servings | Prep time: 15 minutes | Cook time: 15 minutes

Ingredients:
- 1 cup rolled oats
- 3/4 cup whole wheat flour
- 1 1/2 teaspoons ground cinnamon
- 1/2 teaspoon baking soda
- 1/4 teaspoon salt
- 1/4 cup unsalted butter, softened
- 1/4 cup applesauce
- 1/3 cup brown sugar
- 1 large egg
- 1 teaspoon vanilla extract
- 1 medium apple, peeled, cored, and finely chopped

Directions:
1. Preheat oven to 350°F (177°C). Line a baking sheet with parchment paper.
2. In a bowl, whisk together oats, flour, cinnamon, baking soda, and salt.

3. In another bowl, cream together butter, applesauce, and brown sugar until light and fluffy. Beat in the egg and vanilla extract.
4. Gradually add the dry ingredients to the wet ingredients, mixing until just combined. Fold in the chopped apple.
5. Drop tablespoonfuls of the cookie dough onto the prepared baking sheet. Flatten slightly with the back of the spoon.
6. Bake for 12-15 minutes or until cookies are golden and set. Cool on the baking sheet for 5 minutes, then transfer to a wire rack to cool completely.

Nutritional information (approximate per serving):
Calories: 190kcal | Protein: 4g | Carbohydrates: 32g | Fat: 6g | Cholesterol: 35mg | Sodium: 150mg | Fiber: 3g | Potassium: 98mg

Fresh Fruit Compote

Yield: 4 servings | Prep time: 10 minutes | Cook time: 15 minutes

Ingredients:
- 2 cups mixed berries (strawberries, blueberries, raspberries)
- 1 large peach, pitted and sliced
- 1 apple, cored and chopped
- 1/4 cup orange juice
- 2 tablespoons honey
- 1/2 teaspoon ground cinnamon
- 1/4 teaspoon vanilla extract

Directions:
1. In a large saucepan, combine the berries, peach, and apple.
2. Add the orange juice, honey, cinnamon, and vanilla extract.
3. Bring to a simmer over medium heat, then reduce the heat to low and cook for 10-15 minutes, or until the fruit is tender but not mushy.
4. Allow to cool slightly before serving, or chill in the refrigerator to serve cold.

Nutritional information (approximate per serving):
Calories: 120kcal | Protein: 1g | Carbohydrates: 31g | Fat: 0.5g | Cholesterol: 0mg | Sodium: 5mg | Fiber: 5g | Potassium: 212mg

Raspberry Lime Sorbet

Yield: 4 servings | Prep Time: 10 minutes | Cook Time: 0 minutes

Ingredients:
- 3 cups fresh raspberries
- 1/2 cup granulated sugar
- 1/4 cup fresh lime juice
- Zest of 1 lime
- 1/2 cup water

Directions:
1. In a blender, combine raspberries, sugar, lime juice, lime zest, and water. Blend until smooth.
2. Pour the mixture through a fine-mesh sieve into a bowl, pressing on solids to extract as much liquid as possible.
3. Transfer the mixture to an ice cream maker and churn according to manufacturer's instructions, usually about 20-25 minutes.
4. Transfer the sorbet to a freezer-safe container and freeze for at least 4 hours before serving.

Nutritional Information (approximate per serving):
Calories: 120kcal | Protein: 1g | Carbohydrates: 30g | Fat: 0g | Cholesterol: 0mg | Sodium: 0mg | Fiber: 7g | Potassium: 200mg

Agar Fruit Jelly

Yield: 4 servings | Prep Time: 15 minutes | Cook Time: 10 minutes

Ingredients:
- 2 cups mixed fresh fruits (such as strawberries, blueberries, and kiwi), chopped
- 1/4 cup granulated sugar
- 2 cups water
- 2 tablespoons agar agar flakes
- 1 tablespoon lemon juice

Directions:
1. In a saucepan, combine water and agar agar flakes. Bring to a boil, then reduce heat and simmer for 5 minutes, stirring occasionally until the agar agar flakes are completely dissolved.
2. Add sugar to the agar agar mixture, stirring until dissolved. Remove from heat and stir in lemon juice.
3. Arrange the chopped fruits evenly in serving dishes or molds.
4. Pour the agar agar mixture over the fruits.
5. Let it cool to room temperature, then refrigerate for at least 2 hours until set.

Nutritional Information (approximate per serving):
Calories: 80kcal | Protein: 1g | Carbohydrates: 20g | Fat: 0g | Cholesterol: 0mg | Sodium: 5mg | Fiber: 3g | Potassium: 150mg

Pumpkin Mousse

Yield: 4 servings | Prep Time: 15 minutes | Cook Time: 0 minutes

Ingredients:
- 1 cup canned pumpkin puree
- 1/2 cup heavy cream
- 1/4 cup maple syrup
- 1 teaspoon vanilla extract
- 1 teaspoon ground cinnamon
- 1/4 teaspoon ground nutmeg
- 1/4 teaspoon ground ginger
- Whipped cream and cinnamon for garnish (optional)

Directions:
1. In a mixing bowl, combine pumpkin puree, heavy cream, maple syrup, vanilla extract, cinnamon, nutmeg, and ginger.
2. Using a hand mixer or stand mixer, beat the mixture on medium-high speed until smooth and creamy, about 3-5 minutes.
3. Divide the pumpkin mousse evenly among serving dishes.
4. Refrigerate for at least 1 hour before serving.
5. Garnish with whipped cream and a sprinkle of cinnamon, if desired, before serving.

Nutritional Information (approximate per serving):
Calories: 180kcal | Protein: 2g | Carbohydrates: 18g | Fat: 12g | Cholesterol: 41mg | Sodium: 20mg | Fiber: 3g | Potassium: 330mg

Berry and Flaxseed Muffins

Yield: 12 muffins | Prep Time: 15 minutes | Cook Time: 20 minutes

Ingredients:
- 1 1/2 cups all-purpose flour
- 1/2 cup ground flaxseed
- 1/2 cup granulated sugar
- 2 teaspoons baking powder
- 1/2 teaspoon baking soda
- 1/4 teaspoon salt
- 1 cup mixed berries (such as blueberries, raspberries, and blackberries)
- 1 cup buttermilk
- 1/4 cup vegetable oil
- 1 large egg
- 1 teaspoon vanilla extract

Directions:
1. Preheat the oven to 375°F (190°C). Grease or line a muffin tin with paper liners.
2. In a large mixing bowl, combine flour, ground flaxseed, sugar, baking powder, baking soda, and salt.
3. Gently fold in the mixed berries until evenly distributed.
4. In a separate bowl, whisk together buttermilk, vegetable oil, egg, and vanilla extract.
5. Pour the wet ingredients into the dry ingredients and stir until just combined. Do not overmix.
6. Spoon the batter into the prepared muffin tin, filling each cup about 2/3 full.
7. Bake for 18-20 minutes, or until a toothpick inserted into the center of a muffin comes out clean.
8. Allow the muffins to cool in the tin for 5 minutes before transferring them to a wire rack to cool completely.

Nutritional Information (approximate per serving):
Calories: 180kcal | Protein: 4g | Carbohydrates: 25g | Fat: 8g | Cholesterol: 20mg | Sodium: 200mg | Fiber: 3g | Potassium: 150mg

Steamed Apple Pies

Yield: 4 servings | Prep time: 15 minutes | Cook time: 25 minutes

Ingredients:
- 2 cups all-purpose flour
- 1/2 teaspoon salt
- 1/2 cup cold unsalted butter, cubed
- 1/4 cup ice water
- 4 medium-sized apples, peeled, cored, and diced
- 1/4 cup granulated sugar
- 1 teaspoon ground cinnamon
- 1/4 teaspoon ground nutmeg
- 1 tablespoon lemon juice
- 1 tablespoon cornstarch
- Cooking spray or additional butter for greasing

Directions:
1. In a large mixing bowl, combine the flour and salt. Cut in the cold butter using a pastry cutter or fork until the mixture resembles coarse crumbs.
2. Gradually add the ice water, mixing with a fork until the dough comes together. Shape the dough into a ball, wrap it in plastic wrap, and refrigerate for at least 30 minutes.
3. In a separate bowl, toss together the diced apples, granulated sugar, ground cinnamon, ground nutmeg, lemon juice, and cornstarch until well combined.
4. Divide the dough into 8 equal portions. Roll out each portion into a circle on a lightly floured surface.
5. Place a spoonful of the apple mixture onto half of each dough circle. Fold the other half over the filling to form a half-moon shape. Press the edges together to seal, then crimp with a fork.
6. Place the pies onto a greased steamer basket or tray, leaving space between them. Steam for 20-25 minutes until the dough is cooked through and the apples are tender.
7. Serve the steamed apple pies warm, optionally dusted with powdered sugar or served with a scoop of vanilla ice cream.

Nutritional Information (approximate per serving):
Calories: 380kcal | Protein: 4g | Carbohydrates: 52g | Fat: 18g | Cholesterol: 45mg | Sodium: 260mg | Fiber: 4g | Potassium: 210mg

Almond and Coconut Biscotti

Yield: 4 servings | Prep time: 15 minutes | Cook time: 25 minutes

Ingredients:
- 1 cup all-purpose flour
- 1/2 cup granulated sugar
- 1/4 teaspoon baking powder
- 1/4 teaspoon salt
- 1/4 cup unsalted butter, softened
- 1 large egg
- 1/2 teaspoon almond extract
- 1/2 cup shredded coconut
- 1/2 cup chopped almonds

Directions:
1. Preheat your oven to 350°F (175°C). Line a baking sheet with parchment paper.
2. In a mixing bowl, combine flour, sugar, baking powder, and salt. Cut in the softened butter until the mixture resembles coarse crumbs.
3. In a separate bowl, beat the egg with almond extract. Stir this mixture into the dry ingredients until just combined. Fold in the shredded coconut and chopped almonds.
4. Divide the dough in half and shape each half into a log about 9 inches long and 2 inches wide. Place the logs on the prepared baking sheet, leaving space between them.
5. Bake in the preheated oven for 20-25 minutes, or until the logs are firm and lightly browned. Remove from the oven and let cool for 10 minutes. Reduce the oven temperature to 325°F (160°C).

6. Using a sharp knife, cut the logs into 1/2-inch slices. Place the slices cut side down on the baking sheet and bake for an additional 10-15 minutes, or until the biscotti are crisp and golden. Allow them to cool completely before serving.

Nutritional Information (approximate per serving):
Calories: 230kcal | Protein: 4g | Carbohydrates: 26g | Fat: 13g | Cholesterol: 40mg | Sodium: 105mg | Fiber: 2g | Potassium: 130mg

Peach and Berry Cobbler

Yield: 4 servings | Prep time: 15 minutes | Cook time: 30 minutes

Ingredients:
- 2 cups sliced peaches (fresh or frozen)
- 1 cup mixed berries (such as strawberries, blueberries, raspberries)
- 1/4 cup granulated sugar
- 1 tablespoon lemon juice
- 1/2 teaspoon vanilla extract
- 1/2 cup all-purpose flour
- 1/4 cup granulated sugar (for topping)
- 1/2 teaspoon baking powder
- Pinch of salt
- 1/4 cup unsalted butter, melted
- Vanilla ice cream or whipped cream for serving (optional)

Directions:
1. Preheat your oven to 375°F (190°C). Grease a baking dish or skillet with butter or cooking spray.
2. In a large mixing bowl, combine sliced peaches, mixed berries, 1/4 cup sugar, lemon juice, and vanilla extract. Toss until the fruits are coated evenly, then transfer the mixture to the prepared baking dish.
3. In another bowl, whisk together flour, remaining 1/4 cup sugar, baking powder, and salt. Stir in melted butter until the mixture resembles coarse crumbs.
4. Sprinkle the flour mixture evenly over the fruit in the baking dish.
5. Bake in the preheated oven for 25-30 minutes, or until the fruit is bubbling and the topping is golden brown.
6. Allow the cobbler to cool for a few minutes before serving. Serve warm with vanilla ice cream or whipped cream if desired.

Nutritional Information (approximate per serving):
Calories: 280kcal | Protein: 2g | Carbohydrates: 47g | Fat: 10g | Cholesterol: 25mg | Sodium: 70mg | Fiber: 4g | Potassium: 280mg

Mango and Chia Seed Parfait

Yield: 4 servings | Prep time: 10 minutes | Cook time: 0 minutes

Ingredients:
- 2 ripe mangoes, peeled and diced
- 1 cup Greek yogurt
- 1/4 cup chia seeds
- 2 tablespoons honey or maple syrup
- 1/2 teaspoon vanilla extract
- Fresh mint leaves for garnish (optional)

Directions:
1. In a blender or food processor, puree one of the mangoes until smooth. Set aside.
2. In a mixing bowl, combine Greek yogurt, chia seeds, honey or maple syrup, and vanilla extract. Stir well to combine.
3. Layer the parfait glasses or bowls with alternating layers of mango puree, yogurt mixture, and diced mangoes, repeating until all ingredients are used up.
4. Garnish with fresh mint leaves if desired.
5. Serve immediately or refrigerate for at least 30 minutes to allow the flavors to meld together.

Nutritional Information (approximate per serving):
Calories: 200kcal | Protein: 7g | Carbohydrates: 34g | Fat: 5g | Cholesterol: 5mg | Sodium: 35mg | Fiber: 7g | Potassium: 410mg

Pineapple Sorbet

Yield: 4 servings | Prep time: 5 minutes | Cook time: 0 minutes

Ingredients:
- 4 cups frozen pineapple chunks
- 1/4 cup honey or maple syrup
- 1 tablespoon lime juice
- 1/4 cup water

Directions:
1. In a blender or food processor, combine frozen pineapple chunks, honey or maple syrup, lime juice, and water.
2. Blend until smooth and creamy, scraping down the sides of the blender as needed.
3. If the mixture is too thick, you can add a little more water to reach your desired consistency.
4. Once blended, transfer the mixture to a shallow dish and freeze for at least 2 hours, or until firm.
5. Before serving, let the sorbet sit at room temperature for a few minutes to soften slightly. Then, scoop into bowls and enjoy!

Nutritional Information (approximate per serving):
Calories: 110kcal | Protein: 0.5g | Carbohydrates: 29g | Fat: 0g | Cholesterol: 0mg | Sodium: 0mg | Fiber: 2g | Potassium: 180mg

Oatmeal and Raisin Cookies

Yield: 4 servings | Prep time: 15 minutes | Cook time: 12 minutes

Ingredients:
- 1/2 cup unsalted butter, softened
- 1/2 cup packed brown sugar
- 1/4 cup granulated sugar
- 1 large egg
- 1 teaspoon vanilla extract
- 3/4 cup all-purpose flour
- 1/2 teaspoon baking soda
- 1/2 teaspoon ground cinnamon
- 1/4 teaspoon salt
- 1 1/2 cups old-fashioned oats
- 1/2 cup raisins

Directions:
1. Preheat your oven to 350°F (175°C). Line a baking sheet with parchment paper.
2. In a large mixing bowl, cream together the softened butter, brown sugar, and granulated sugar until light and fluffy.
3. Beat in the egg and vanilla extract until well combined.
4. In a separate bowl, whisk together the flour, baking soda, cinnamon, and salt. Gradually add the dry ingredients to the wet ingredients and mix until just combined.
5. Stir in the oats and raisins until evenly distributed throughout the dough.
6. Drop rounded tablespoonfuls of dough onto the prepared baking sheet, spacing them about 2 inches apart. Flatten each cookie slightly with the back of a spoon.
7. Bake in the preheated oven for 10-12 minutes, or until the edges are golden brown. Allow the cookies to cool on the baking sheet for a few minutes before transferring them to a wire rack to cool completely.

Nutritional Information (approximate per serving):
Calories: 310kcal | Protein: 4g | Carbohydrates: 42g | Fat: 14g | Cholesterol: 65mg | Sodium: 210mg | Fiber: 2g | Potassium: 190mg

Baked Apples with Cinnamon

Yield: 4 servings | Prep time: 10 minutes | Cook time: 30 minutes

Ingredients:
- 4 medium apples (such as Granny Smith or Honeycrisp)
- 2 tablespoons unsalted butter, melted
- 2 tablespoons brown sugar
- 1 teaspoon ground cinnamon
- 1/4 cup chopped nuts (optional)
- Vanilla ice cream or whipped cream for serving (optional)

Directions:
1. Preheat your oven to 375°F (190°C). Grease a baking dish with butter or cooking spray.
2. Core the apples and place them in the prepared baking dish.
3. In a small bowl, mix the melted butter, brown sugar, and ground cinnamon.
4. Spoon the butter mixture evenly over each apple, making sure to coat them well.
5. If using chopped nuts, sprinkle them over the top of each apple.
6. Bake in the preheated oven for 25-30 minutes, or until the apples are tender and the topping is golden brown.
7. Serve the baked apples warm, optionally topped with vanilla ice cream or whipped cream.

Nutritional Information (approximate per serving):
Calories: 180kcal | Protein: 1g | Carbohydrates: 28g | Fat: 9g | Cholesterol: 15mg | Sodium: 0mg | Fiber: 5g | Potassium: 210mg

Pumpkin and Spice Pudding

Yield: 4 servings | Prep time: 10 minutes | Cook time: 10 minutes

Ingredients:
- 1 cup canned pumpkin puree
- 1/4 cup brown sugar
- 1 teaspoon pumpkin pie spice
- 1/2 teaspoon ground cinnamon
- 1/4 teaspoon ground nutmeg
- 1/4 teaspoon ground ginger
- Pinch of salt
- 1 cup whole milk
- 2 tablespoons cornstarch
- 1 teaspoon vanilla extract
- Whipped cream or chopped nuts for garnish (optional)

Directions:
1. In a saucepan, combine the pumpkin puree, brown sugar, pumpkin pie spice, cinnamon, nutmeg, ginger, and salt. Cook over medium heat, stirring constantly, for 2-3 minutes until heated through and fragrant.
2. In a small bowl, whisk together the milk and cornstarch until smooth. Pour the milk mixture into the saucepan with the pumpkin mixture, stirring continuously.
3. Cook the mixture over medium heat, stirring constantly, until it thickens and comes to a gentle boil, about 5 minutes.
4. Remove the saucepan from the heat and stir in the vanilla extract.
5. Divide the pudding into serving dishes and refrigerate for at least 2 hours, or until chilled and set.
6. Serve the pumpkin and spice pudding chilled, topped with whipped cream or chopped nuts if desired.

Nutritional Information (approximate per serving):
Calories: 140kcal | Protein: 3g | Carbohydrates: 25g | Fat: 3g | Cholesterol: 5mg | Sodium: 80mg | Fiber: 3g | Potassium: 32

Vanilla and Berry Yogurt Pops

Yield: 4 servings | Prep time: 10 minutes | Cook time: 0 minutes

Ingredients:
- 1 cup Greek yogurt
- 1 tablespoon honey or maple syrup
- 1 teaspoon vanilla extract
- 1/2 cup mixed berries (such as strawberries, blueberries, raspberries)

Directions:
1. In a mixing bowl, combine Greek yogurt, honey or maple syrup, and vanilla extract. Stir until well combined.
2. Gently fold in the mixed berries until evenly distributed throughout the yogurt mixture.
3. Spoon the yogurt and berry mixture into popsicle molds, filling each mold to the top.
4. Insert popsicle sticks into the molds and freeze for at least 4 hours, or until completely frozen.

5. Once frozen, run the popsicle molds under warm water for a few seconds to loosen the popsicles before removing them from the molds.

Nutritional Information (approximate per serving):
Calories: 70kcal | Protein: 4g | Carbohydrates: 10g | Fat: 1g | Cholesterol: 5mg | Sodium: 20mg | Fiber: 1g | Potassium: 100mg

From the writer

As we close the pages of "Low Cholesterol Cookbook: 2000 Days of Heart-Healthy Habits and Easy Quick Recipes with Simple Ingredients," I hope you've discovered not just a collection of recipes, but a gateway to a healthier, more vibrant life. This journey we've embarked on together is about more than lowering cholesterol—it's about embracing a lifestyle that nourishes the heart in every way.

I've shared with you the lessons learned on my own path to wellness, hoping to inspire and empower you to take control of your health. Each recipe, each piece of advice, is a step towards a life filled with joy, vitality, and delicious, heart-healthy meals.

But our journey doesn't have to end here. I'd be thrilled if you could take a moment to share your experiences with this cookbook on Amazon. Your feedback not only supports me but also guides others on their path to heart health. Whether it's a story of transformation, a favorite recipe that's become a staple in your kitchen, or suggestions for future editions, I welcome your thoughts. Let's continue to support each other in our quest for a healthy heart and a fulfilled life.

The link for the review is at Amazon.com

https://www.amazon.com/review/create-review/error?ie=UTF8&channel=glance-detail&asin=B0CY2WK8WQ

email me if you would like photos of the dishes or clarification on preparation!

savoryariana@gmail.com

With love and gratitude,
          Ariana Elizabeth Montgomery

Meal plan

28 days

	Breakfast	Lunch	Dinner	Snack	Nutrition Information
Day 1	Fresh Pineapple (150 kcal)	Kale and Quinoa Salad with Lemon-Tahini Dressing (300 kcal) + Classic Vegetable Soup (120 kcal)	Oven-Roasted Turkey Breast (300 kcal)	Greek Yogurt with Mixed Berries (200 kcal) + Almond Berry Banana Boost (180 kcal)	1250kcal
Day 2	Avocado Toast with Black Pepper (200 kcal)	Spinach and Berry Salad with Poppy Seed Dressing (250 kcal) + Butternut Squash Soup (180 kcal)	Chicken Kebabs with Vegetables (350 kcal)	Peanut Butter Cup Protein Shake (200 kcal)	1180 kcal
Day 3	Nut and Seed Granola with Almond Milk (300 kcal)	Mediterranean Chickpea Salad with Herb Dressing (350 kcal) + Tomato Basil Soup (220 kcal)	Grilled Lemon Herb Chicken Breast (300 kcal)	Berry Spinach Surprise (150 kcal)	1320kcal
Day 4	Creamy Oat Banana Pancakes (250 kcal)	Avocado and Black Bean Salad with Cilantro-Lime Dressing (350 kcal) + Chickpea and Spinach Soup (190 kcal)	Baked Beef Steak with Herbs (350 kcal)	Classic Hummus with Whole-Wheat Crackers (150 kcal)	1290kcal
Day 5	Steel-Cut Oats with Almond Slivers and Peach Slices (300 kcal)	Crunchy Cabbage Slaw with Sesame Ginger Dressing (250 kcal) + Creamy Potato	Balsamic Glazed Chicken Breast (350 kcal)	Avocado Chocolate Smoothie with Almonds (200 kcal)	1360 kcal

		Leek Soup (260 kcal)			
Day 6	Egg White Veggie Scramble (200 kcal)	Greek Salad with Herb Marinated Olives (300 kcal) + Mushroom Barley Soup (240 kcal)	Turkey Patties with Oats (300 kcal)	Fruit Kabobs with Yogurt Dip (200 kcal	1240kcal
Day 7	Chia Seed Pudding with Almond Milk and Mixed Berries (250 kcal)	Cucumber Tomato Salad with Cilantro and Lime (200 kcal) + Spicy Black Bean Soup (200 kcal	Grilled Chicken with Avocado Salsa (350 kcal)	Green Tea Smoothie with Mint and Lemon (150 kcal)	1150kcal
Day 8	Breakfast Quinoa with Apples and Walnuts (214 kcal)	Vegetarian Niçoise Salad (350 kcal) + Classic Vegetable Soup (120 kcal)	Chicken Thighs with Rosemary and Garlic (350 kcal)	Celery Sticks with Peanut Butter (150 kcal)	1184kcal
Day 9	Pumpkin Spice Oatmeal (300 kcal)	Lentil and Vegetable Stew (350 kcal) + Creamy Potato Leek Soup (260 kcal)	Beef Stir-Fry with Broccoli and Bell Peppers (400 kcal)	Almond Berry Banana Boost (190 kcal)	1500kcal
Day 10	Sweet Potato and Kale Breakfast Hash (300 kcal)	Cucumber Yogurt Salad (200 kcal) + Butternut Squash Soup (180 kcal)	Roasted Chicken Quarters with Herbs and Root Vegetables (400 kcal)	Greek Yogurt with Mixed Berries (200 kcal)	1280kcal
Day 11	Cauliflower Rice Porridge (240 kcal)	Greek Salad with Herb Marinated Olives (300 kcal) + Tomato Basil Soup (220 kcal	Meatballs in Marinara Sauce over Zucchini Noodles (400 kcal)	Berry Spinach Surprise (150 kcal)	1310kcal
Day 12	Zucchini Bread Oatmeal (300 kcal)	Broccoli Cranberry Salad (250 kcal) + Golden Lentil and Spinach Soup (240 kcal)	Herb-Roasted Lamb Leg with Mint Yogurt Sauce (400 kcal	Avocado Chocolate Smoothie with Almonds (200 kcal)	1390kcal

Day 13	Tofu and Vegetable Breakfast Tacos (230 kcal)	Warm Cauliflower Salad (250 kcal) + Mushroom Barley Soup (240 kcal)	Turkey Meatloaf with Zucchini (350 kcal)	Fruit Kabobs with Yogurt Dip (200 kcal)	1270kcal
Day 14	Almond and Blueberry Breakfast Smoothie (270 kcal)	Arugula and Pear Salad (300 kcal) + Creamy Broccoli and Cauliflower Soup (220 kcal)	Balsamic Glazed Chicken Breast (350 kcal)	Multigrain Berry Bar (180 kcal)	1320kcal
Day 15	Almond Berry Banana Boost (180 kcal)	Vegetarian Niçoise Salad (350 kcal) + Carrot Ginger Soup (220 kcal)	Spiced Lean Pork Tenderloin (450 kcal)	Classic Hummus with Whole-Wheat Crackers (150 kcal)	1350kcal
Day 15	Almond Berry Banana Boost (180 kcal)	Vegetarian Niçoise Salad (350 kcal) + Carrot Ginger Soup (220 kcal)	Spiced Lean Pork Tenderloin (450 kcal)	Classic Hummus with Whole-Wheat Crackers (150 kcal)	1350kcal
Day 17	Zucchini Bread Oatmeal (300 kcal)	Cucumber Yogurt Salad (200 kcal) + White Bean Puree Soup with Pumpkin and Ginger (300 kcal)	Chicken Zucchini Skewers (290 kcal)	Edamame Hummus Wrap (200 kcal)	1290kcal
Day 18	Tofu and Vegetable Breakfast Tacos (230 kcal)	Broccoli Cranberry Salad (250 kcal) + Lemon Cucumber Soup with Cilantro, Olives, and Capers (220 kcal)	Seared Scallops with Sweet Corn Puree (420 kcal)	Peanut Butter and Banana Roll-Ups (200 kcal)	1320kcal
Day 19	Coconut Milk Chia Pudding with Nuts and Dried Fruits (250 kcal)	Greek Salad with Herb Marinated Olives (300 kcal) + Spicy Black Bean Soup (240 kcal)	Turkey Chili with Beans and Vegetables (320 kcal)	Berry Keto Smoothie with Raspberry and Coconut Milk (200 kcal)	1310kcal
Day 20	Egg White and Salmon Roll-Ups (180 kcal)	Summer Berry Spinach Salad with Honey Lime	Herb-Crusted Halibut (400 kcal)	Vegetable Spring Rolls (172 kcal)	1292kcal

		Dressing (300 kcal) + Golden Lentil and Spinach Soup (240 kcal)			
Day 21	Cauliflower Rice Porridge (240 kcal)	Tomato Basil Mozzarella Salad (350 kcal) + Sweet Corn and Zucchini Soup (250 kcal)	Baked Chicken Thighs with Rosemary and Garlic (350 kcal)	Green Tea Smoothie with Mint and Lemon (150 kcal)	1340kcal
Day 22	Coconut Milk Chia Pudding with Nuts and Dried Fruits (200 kcal)	Vegetarian Niçoise Salad (350 kcal) + Spicy Mustard Sauce (50 kcal) + Cabbage Soup with Beans and Tomatoes (200 kcal)	Mediterranean Turkey Burgers (400 kcal)	Almond Berry Banana Boost (180 kcal) + Classic Guacamole (120 kcal)	1500kcal
Day 23	Egg White and Salmon Roll-Ups (180 kcal)	Arugula and Pear Salad (300 kcal) + Lemon Ginger Sauce (50 kcal) + Onion Soup with Potato and Carrot (200 kcal)	Grilled Chicken with Avocado Salsa (350 kcal)	Peanut Butter and Banana Roll-Ups (220 kcal) + Spinach and Feta Stuffed Mushrooms (100 kcal)	1400kcal
Day 24	Buckwheat Pancakes with Fresh Berries and Maple Syrup (235 kcal)	Crunchy Cabbage Slaw with Sesame Ginger Dressing (250 kcal) + Golden Turmeric Tahini Sauce (60 kcal) + Creamy Dill Sauce (50 kcal) + Tomato Cocktail Soup with Shrimp and Avocado (200 kcal)	Spiced Lean Pork Tenderloin (450 kcal)	Vegetable Spring Rolls (172 kcal) + Fresh Pineapple (100 kcal)	1517kcal
Day 25	Baked Oatmeal Squares with Apple Slices and Pecans (280 kcal)	Chickpea Salad with Herb Dressing (350 kcal) + Broiled Cod with Tomato Basil Salsa (300 kcal)	Herb-Crusted Lamb Chops (400 kcal)	Avocado Berry Smoothie (210 kcal)	1540kcal

Day 26	Nut and Seed Granola with Almond Milk (380 kcal)	Mixed Greens with Apple and Walnut Vinaigrette (300 kcal) + White Garlic Bean Soup (220 kcal)	Braised Turkey with Vegetables and Lentils (400 kcal)	Multigrain Berry Bar (150 kcal)	1450kcal
Day 27	Vegan Tofu Scramble with Turmeric, Bell Peppers, Onions, and Spinach (146 kcal)	Warm Cauliflower Salad (250 kcal) + Mango Avocado Salsa (60 kcal) + Artichoke Soup with Spinach (200 kcal)	Turkey Chili with Beans and Vegetables (350 kcal)	Green Almond Energizer Smoothie (150 kcal) + Red Currant Jelly (60 kcal) on whole grain toast (70 kcal)	1286kcal
Day 28	Pumpkin Spice Oatmeal (300 kcal)	Tomato Basil Mozzarella Salad (350 kcal) + Balsamic Reduction (50 kcal) + Carrot Ginger Soup (220 kcal)	Lemon Garlic Shrimp Skewers with Asparagus (400 kcal)	Berry and Flaxseed Muffins (180 kcal)	1500kcal

Shopping List

Proteins:
- Turkey breast
- Chicken breasts
- Ground turkey
- Beef steak
- Chicken thighs
- Eggs

Dairy and Dairy Alternatives:
- Greek yogurt
- Almond milk
- Cheese (if needed for recipes)

Fruits:
- Mixed berries (for yogurt, smoothies, and snacks)
- Bananas
- Peaches
- Apples
- Lemons

Vegetables:
- Avocados
- Spinach
- Butternut squash
- Tomatoes
- Cucumbers
- Carrots
- Cabbage
- Potatoes
- Leeks
- Mushrooms
- Broccoli
- Bell peppers
- Celery

Grains, Nuts, and Seeds:
- Whole wheat bread
- Quinoa
- Oats
- Walnuts
- Almonds
- Chia seeds
- Whole-wheat crackers
- Barley

Legumes:
- Chickpeas
- Black beans
- Lentils

Herbs, Spices, and Condiments for Dressings and Meals:
- Olive oil
- Vinegar (balsamic, red wine, or white wine for dressings)
- Garlic
- Fresh herbs (basil, cilantro, rosemary, mint)
- Dried herbs and spices (poppy seeds, sesame seeds, black pepper, salt, pumpkin spice mix, etc.)
- Peanut butter
- Honey or another sweetener
- Mustard
- Lime
- Ginger

Additional Items:
- Protein powder (for protein shakes)
- Hummus

Part 5: Sustaining Heart-Healthy Habits

As you embark on your journey to lower cholesterol and maintain a heart-healthy lifestyle, it's crucial to establish sustainable habits that will support your long-term well-being. In this section, we'll explore strategies for sticking with your new eating habits, adjusting your diet as your health and nutritional needs change, and incorporating physical activity into your daily routine.

Strategies for Sticking with Your New Eating Habits

Changing your eating habits can be challenging, but with the right strategies, you can make lasting changes that benefit your heart health. Here are some tips to help you stay on track:

1. Set Realistic Goals: Start by setting achievable goals for yourself. Break larger goals into smaller, manageable steps, and celebrate your progress along the way.

2. Plan: Take time to plan your meals and snacks for the week ahead. Stock your kitchen with heart-healthy ingredients and prepare meals in advance to avoid the temptation of unhealthy options.

3. Find Healthy Swaps: Explore healthier alternatives to your favorite foods, such as swapping saturated fats for unsaturated fats, or choosing whole grains over refined grains.

4. Stay Mindful: Practice mindful eating by paying attention to your hunger and fullness cues. Avoid distractions while eating and savor each bite to fully enjoy your food.

5. Seek Support: Surround yourself with a supportive network of friends, family, or a healthcare professional who can offer encouragement and guidance on your journey to better health.

Adjusting Your Diet as Your Health and Nutritional Needs Change

1. Regularly Monitor Your Health: Stay proactive about monitoring your cholesterol levels and overall health. Work with your healthcare provider to assess your progress and make any necessary adjustments to your diet.

2. Stay Informed: Keep up to date with the latest research and recommendations on heart-healthy eating. Stay informed about new foods, cooking techniques, and nutritional guidelines that can benefit your health.

3. Listen to Your Body: Pay attention to how your body responds to different foods and dietary changes. Adjust your diet based on your individual needs and preferences.

4. Consult a Registered Dietitian: If you're unsure how to adjust your diet to meet your changing needs, consider consulting a registered dietitian. They can provide personalized guidance and support to help you optimize your nutrition.

Incorporating Physical Activity into a Heart-Healthy Lifestyle

In addition to a healthy diet, regular physical activity is essential for maintaining heart health. Here are some tips for incorporating exercise into your daily routine:

1. Find Activities You Enjoy: Choose activities that you genuinely enjoy, whether it's walking, swimming, cycling, or dancing. Finding activities,

you love will make it easier to stick with your exercise routine.

2. Start Slowly: If you're new to exercise or have been inactive for a while, start slowly and gradually increase the intensity and duration of your workouts. Aim for at least 150 minutes of moderate-intensity exercise per week.

3. Stay Consistent: Make exercise a regular part of your routine by scheduling it into your day. Aim for consistency rather than intensity, and find opportunities to be active throughout the day, such as taking the stairs or going for a walk during your lunch break.

4. Mix It Up: Keep your workouts interesting by trying different activities and varying your routine. Incorporating a mix of cardiovascular exercise, strength training, and flexibility exercises will help you stay fit and prevent boredom.

By implementing these strategies for sustaining heart-healthy habits, you can support your long-term health and well-being while enjoying a fulfilling and vibrant life. Remember that small changes can lead to significant improvements in your heart health, so stay committed and celebrate your successes along the way.

Appendices

Glossary of Terms Related to Cholesterol and Heart Health

1. Cholesterol: A waxy substance found in the blood that is essential for building cell membranes and producing hormones, but high levels can increase the risk of heart disease.

2. LDL (Low-Density Lipoprotein): Often referred to as "bad" cholesterol, LDL carries cholesterol from the liver to cells but can deposit it in artery walls, leading to atherosclerosis.

3. HDL (High-Density Lipoprotein): Known as "good" cholesterol, HDL helps remove LDL cholesterol from the bloodstream and transport it to the liver for excretion.

4. Atherosclerosis: A condition characterized by the buildup of plaque, consisting of cholesterol, fat, and other substances, on the walls of arteries, narrowing and hardening them.

5. Triglycerides: A type of fat found in the blood that stores excess energy from the diet and contributes to atherosclerosis when levels are high.

6. Coronary Artery Disease (CAD): A condition caused by atherosclerosis in the coronary arteries, leading to reduced blood flow to the heart and an increased risk of heart attack.

7. Myocardial Infarction (Heart Attack): Occurs when blood flow to part of the heart muscle is blocked, usually by a blood clot, resulting in tissue damage or death.

8. Hypertension (High Blood Pressure: A condition characterized by elevated blood pressure levels, which can strain the heart and increase the risk of cardiovascular disease.

9.Stroke: A sudden interruption of blood flow to the brain, either due to a blockage (ischemic stroke) or bleeding (hemorrhagic stroke), resulting in brain damage or death.

10. Cardiovascular Disease (CVD): A group of conditions affecting the heart and blood vessels, including coronary artery disease, stroke, and peripheral artery disease.

11. Risk Factors: Factors or conditions that increase the likelihood of developing heart disease, such as high cholesterol, high blood pressure, smoking, obesity, and physical inactivity.

12. Dietary Fiber: Indigestible plant material found in fruits, vegetables, whole grains, and legumes that can help lower cholesterol levels and improve heart health.

13. Omega-3 Fatty Acids: Essential fatty acids found in fatty fish (such as salmon and mackerel), flaxseeds, and walnuts, which have been shown to reduce triglyceride levels and decrease the risk of heart disease.

14. Statins: Medications that lower cholesterol levels by inhibiting the enzyme involved in cholesterol production in the liver, commonly prescribed to reduce the risk of heart attack and stroke.

15. Exercise: Physical activity that strengthens the heart and improves circulation, reducing the risk of heart disease and promoting overall cardiovascular health.

Nutritional Information and Resources

1. Nutritional Information
  - Macronutrients: Learn about the three main macronutrients: carbohydrates, proteins, and fats, and their roles in the body. - Micronutrients : Explore essential vitamins and minerals required for various bodily functions and overall health.
  - Dietary Fiber: Understand the importance of dietary fiber in digestion, satiety, and maintaining a healthy gut microbiome.
  - Healthy Eating Guidelines: Discover dietary recommendations from reputable health organizations, such as the USDA Dietary Guidelines for Americans or the World Health Organization's nutrition guidelines.

2. Label Reading and Portion Control

  - Nutrition Labels : Gain proficiency in reading and interpreting nutrition labels to make informed food choices at the grocery store.
  - Portion Control: Learn strategies for managing portion sizes to prevent overeating and maintain a balanced diet.

3. Meal Planning and Healthy Cooking

  - Meal Planning: Explore tips and techniques for meal planning, including batch cooking, creating balanced meals, and incorporating variety.
  - Healthy Cooking Methods: Discover healthier cooking methods, such as grilling, steaming, and baking, to retain nutrients while minimizing added fats and calories.

4. Nutritional Resources

  - Online Resources: Access reputable websites, such as government health agencies, academic institutions, and nutrition-focused organizations, for evidence-based nutrition information.
  - Mobile Applications: Explore nutrition-related apps that offer meal tracking, recipe ideas, and personalized dietary recommendations.
  - Books and Cookbooks: Explore a selection of books and cookbooks authored by nutrition experts, dietitians, and chefs, offering guidance on healthy eating and culinary inspiration.

5. Additional Support
  - Registered Dietitians: Consider seeking guidance from a registered dietitian for personalized nutrition counseling and support in achieving your health goals.
  - Community Resources: Explore local community programs, support groups, and wellness centers that offer nutrition education, cooking classes, and other resources to support healthy lifestyles.

Measurement Conversion Table

Volume Conversions:
- 1 tablespoon (tbsp) = 3 teaspoons (tsp)
- 1 cup = 16 tablespoons
- 1 cup = 8 fluid ounces (fl oz)
- 1 pint (pt.) = 2 cups
- 1 quart (qt) = 2 pints
- 1 gallon (gal) = 4 quarts
- 1 litter (L) = 4.22675 cups

Weight Conversions:
- 1 ounce (oz) = 28.3495 grams (g)
- 1 pound (lb) = 16 ounces
- 1 kilogram (kg) = 2.20462 pounds

Temperature Conversions (approximate):
- 32°F = 0°C (freezing point of water)
- 212°F = 100°C (boiling point of water)
- To convert from Fahrenheit to Celsius: (°F - 32) × 5/9 = °C
- To convert from Celsius to Fahrenheit: (°C × 9/5) + 32 = °F

Length Conversions:
- 1 inch (in) = 2.54 centimetres (cm)

Index:

-A-
- Almond and Blueberry Breakfast Smoothie 27
- Almond Berry Banana Boost 34
- Almond Butter and Banana on Whole Grain Bread 16
- Apple Cinnamon Oat Cookies 90
- Apple Cinnamon Porridge 23
- Avocado Berry Smoothie 22
- Avocado Bracket Bowl 15
- Avocado Caprese Salad 43
- Avocado Chocolate Pudding 90
- Avocado Chocolate Smoothie with Almonds 29
- Avocado Cilantro Lime Sauce 55
- Avocado Toast with Black Pepper 14
- Avocado Toast with Tomato Salsa 33

-B-
- Baked Apples with Cinnamon 95
- Baked Beef Steak with Herbs 61
- Baked Cod with Olive Tapenade 81
- Baked Cod with Tomatoes, Olives, and Capers 76
- Baked Oatmeal Squares with Apple Slices and Pecans 21
- Baked Salmon with Dill and Lemon 71
- Baked Salmon with Green Vegetables 70
- Baked Sweet Potato Filled with Black Beans, Corn, and Avocado Salsa 20
- Baked Tuna Carpaccio 71
- Barley and Apple Porridge 24
- Barley and Mushroom Stew 50
- Basil Pesto with Walnuts 55
- Berry and Flaxseed Muffins 92
- Berry Beet Smoothie 36
- Berry Keto Smoothie with Raspberry and Coconut Milk 30
- Berry Spinach Surprise: Mixed Berries, Spinach, and Chia Seeds 29
- Black Bean and Corn Tacos 80
- Black Bean and Sweet Potato Chili 83
- Blueberry Almond Antioxidant Smoothie 34
- Braised Turkey with Vegetables and Lentils 63
- Breakfast Quinoa with Apples and Walnuts 25
- Broccoli Cranberry Salad 42
- Broiled Cod with Tomato Basil Salsa 72
- Buckwheat Pancakes with Berry Sause 88
- Buckwheat Pancakes with Fresh Berries and Maple Syrup 20
- Butternut Squash Soup 44

-C-
- Cabbage Soup with Beans and Tomatoes 51
- Carrot and Apple Loaf 87
- Carrot Ginger Soup 47
- Carrot Ginger Turmeric Smoothie 36
- Cauliflower Rice Porridge 26
- Cauliflower Soup with Broccoli and Potato 53
- Celery Sticks with Peanut Butter 27
- Chickpea and Quinoa Salad 39

- Chickpea and Spinach Soup 45
- Chia Seed Pudding with Almond Milk and Mixed Berries 17
- Chimichurri Sauce 57
- Cinnamon Apple Almond Smoothie 34
- Cinnamon Apple Chips 89
- Classic Guacamole 31
- Classic Hummus with Whole-Wheat Crackers 30
- Classic Vegetable Soup 44
- Coconut Milk Chia Pudding with Nuts and Dried Fruits 15
- Cottage Cheese Pudding with Vanilla 88
- Cottage Cheese with Fresh Pineapple 13
- Creamy Avocado Smoothie 28
- Creamy Broccoli and Cauliflower Soup 46
- Creamy Dill Sauce 58
- Creamy Oat Banana Pancakes 14
- Creamy Potato Leek Soup 46
- Crunchy Cabbage Slaw with Sesame Ginger Dressing 38
- Cucumber Dill Yogurt Sauce 59
- Cucumber Hummus Bite 32
- Cucumber Yogurt Salad 42

-E-
- Egg White and Salmon Roll-Ups 23
- Egg White Veggie Scramble 16
- Edamame Hummus Wrap 84

-F-
- Fruit Kabobs with Yogurt Dip 32
- Fruit Salad with Yogurt: 86

-G-
- Garlic Roasted Cauliflower Steaks 79
- Golden Lentil and Spinach Soup 47
- Golden Turmeric Tahini Sauce 56
- Greek Salad with Herb Marinated Olives 39
- Greek Yogurt with Honey, Walnuts, and Sliced Strawberries 17
- Greek Yogurt with Mixed Berries 28
- Green Almond Energizer Smoothie 35
- Green Matcha Smoothie 36
- Green Tea Smoothie with Mint and Lemon 30
- Grilled Chicken with Avocado Salsa 64
- Grilled Lemon Garlic Shrimp Skewers 72
- Grilled Lemon Herb Chicken Breast 60
- Grilled Mahi Mahi with Pineapple Salsa 73
- Grilled Salmon with Dill and Lemon 75
- Grilled Swordfish with Mango Salsa 72
- Grilled Tuna Steaks with Mango Salsa 73

-H-
- Herb-Baked Tilapia with Lemon Quinoa 73
- Herb-Crusted Lamb Chops 62
- Herb-Roasted Lamb Leg with Mint Yogurt Sauce 67

-L-
- Lemon Cucumber Soup with Cilantro, Olives, and Capers 50
- Lemon Garlic Shrimp Skewers with Asparagus 75
- Lemon Ginger Sauce 57
- Lentil and Vegetable Stew 78
- Lentil and Walnut Burgers 82
- Low-fat Horseradish Sauce 57

-M-
- Mango Avocado Salad with Honey Lime Dressing 40
- Mango-Banana Green Smoothie 35
- Mediterranean Chickpea Salad with Herb Dressing 38
- Mediterranean Turkey Burgers 63
- Miso Soup with Tofu and Seaweed 48
- Mixed Greens with Apple and Walnut Vinaigrette 38
- Multigrain Berry Bar 31
- Mushroom Barley Soup 45

-N-
- Nut and Seed Granola with Almond Milk 15

-O-
- Oat Soup with Vegetables and Shrimp 52
- Oatmeal and Raisin Cookies 95
- Overnight Oats with Chia Seeds, Almond Milk, and Blueberries 18
- Overnight Oats with Fruit 13

-P-
- Peanut Butter and Banana Roll-Ups 31
- Peanut Butter Cup Protein Shake 29
- Peanut Ginger Sauce 55
- Pear Crumble with Oat Topping 87
- Peach and Berry Cobbler 94

- Peanut Ginger Sauce 55
- Pineapple Coconut Smoothie 36
- Pineapple Sorbet 95
- Pumpkin and Spice Pudding 96
- Pumpkin Mousse 92
- Pumpkin Spice Oatmeal 25

-Q-
- Quinoa Breakfast Bowl with Sliced Almonds, Banana, and Cinnamon 19
- Quinoa Breakfast Bowls 23
- Quinoa Stuffed Bell Peppers 78

-R-
- Raspberry Lime Sorbet 91
- Red Currant Jelly 88
- Roasted Beet and Goat Cheese Salad with Balsamic Reduction 39
- Roasted Chickpeas 28
- Roasted Chicken Quarters with Herbs and Root Vegetables 66
- Roasted Garlic Sauce 59
- Rosemary Chicken and Potatoes 63

-S-
- Sautéed Shrimp with Garlic and Lemon 71
- Seared Scallops with Sweet Corn Puree 75
- Seitan Beef Stew 83
- Spinach and Berry Salad with Poppy Seed Dressing 37
- Spinach and Feta Stuffed Mushrooms 33
- Spinach Pineapple Smoothie Bowl with Banana and Flaxseeds 20
- Spiced Lean Pork Tenderloin 68
- Spicy Black Bean Soup 49
- Spicy Grilled Shrimp with Yogurt Sauce 76
- Spicy Mustard Sauce 58
- Spinach Pineapple Smoothie Bowl with Banana and Flaxseeds 20
- Steel-Cut Oats with Almond Slivers and Peach Slices 17
- Steamed Apple Pies 93
- Steamed Fish with Lemon and Herbs 70
- Strawberry Tiramisu Without Sugar 89
- Stuffed Chicken Breasts with Spinach and Mushrooms 61
- Stuffed Eggplant with Lentils 82
- Summer Berry Spinach Salad with Honey Lime Dressing 39
- Sweet Corn and Zucchini Soup 49
- Sweet Potato and Kale Breakfast Hash 26
- Sweet Potato Hash with Black Beans and Avocado 18

-T-
- Tempeh Bacon BLT 84
- Tilapia Tacos with Cabbage Slaw 77
- Tomato Basil Mozzarella Salad 41
- Tomato Basil Soup 45
- Tomato Cocktail Soup with Shrimp and Avocado 53
- Tofu and Broccoli Stir-Fry 79
- Tofu and Vegetable Breakfast Tacos 24
- Tofu Stir-Fry with Vegetables 82
- Tropical Almond Delight Smoothie 35
- Turkey Chili with Beans and Vegetables 64
- Turkey Meatballs in Marinara Sauce over Zucchini Noodles 66
- Turkey Meatloaf with Zucchini 67
- Turkey Patties with Oats 61
- Turmeric-Ginger Baked Chicken 62

-V-
- Vanilla and Berry Yogurt Pops 94
- Vegan Blueberry Muffins with Oat Milk and Coconut Oil 19
- Vegan Meatloaf with Lentils and Mushrooms 85
- Vegan Tofu Scramble with Turmeric, Bell Peppers, Onions, and Spinach 21
- Vegetable Quinoa Soup 48
- Vegetable Spring Rolls 33
- Vegetarian Chili with Quinoa 80
- Vegetarian Niçoise Salad 43
- Veggie Breakfast Tacos 22

-W-
- Warm Cauliflower Salad 42
- Whole Grain Toast with Ricotta Cheese and Sliced Pears 18

-Z-
- Zucchini Bread Oatmeal 25
- Zucchini Noodles with Pesto 81